The Meaning of the American Revolution

The Meaning of the American Revolution

Edited with an Introduction by
Lawrence H. Leder

☙ a New York Times Book

Quadrangle Books
CHICAGO

Contents

2. The Revolution's Creativity

3. The Revolution as a Continuing Process

4. The Other Side

The Meaning of the American Revolution

Introduction

THE PAST eternally impinges on the present and conditions men's responses to their problems. In assessing contemporary society, the American Revolution figures prominently because it is an inexhaustible reservoir of ideas which offers comfort or ammunition to those who hold differing viewpoints.

The variety of interpretations of the American Revolution results from the cataclysmic nature of the event. Any revolution is a complex of many strands and themes, and to comprehend all of them is well-nigh impossible. Each generation of scholars has taken a different approach to the upheaval of 1776, thus giving it a multi-dimensional nature, but no one has offered a final and definitive answer as to why it occurred or what it meant. Our understanding has been expanded with each new explanation, but like all great events the American Revolution remains an elusive quantity.

Certainly one approach to the Revolution was suggested during the event by John Adams. He noted that it began not in 1763 or 1776, but in the minds of men early in the eighteenth century. Americans and Englishmen had in fact become two separate peoples, and by the 1760's American life-styles, thought patterns, and societal goals no longer conformed to those of Englishmen. Some colonists still looked to England for guidance and leadership, but without realizing it they had drifted out of the main stream of American life and would after 1776 make up the bulk of those who could not accept independence. Clearly, 1776 pinpointed America's acceptance of its own destiny.

Historians have traditionally looked back to 1763 and the Anglo-American victory in the French and Indian War for the beginnings of the imperial crisis. Until then, relatively tranquil relations existed between colonies and mother country, for both saw the need to cooperate in the lengthy conflict with France that began in 1688.

France's expulsion from North America in 1763 changed everything. England and America no longer had a common enemy, and disagreements that had previously been submerged now came into the open. For example, England had incurred an enormous debt, had unsuccessfully sought colonial financial help during the war, and now could force colonial assistance. Imperial controls had been neglected while England sought colonial cooperation, but now the mother country could give closer attention to such matters. And Canada's acquisition presented both England and America with new problems which demanded immediate resolution, but for which there were no easy answers.

Thus England, faced with the fruits of victory, found them bitter. Everyone expected tranquility, but peace produced arguments, conflicts, and disunity. The new problems demonstrated the inadequacy of the cumbersome British administrative system and its moribund and rigid policy-makers. Britain found itself unable to accept or accommodate changes which had occurred in America during the past seventy-five years.

Americans for generations had prided themselves on being Englishmen, but now they challenged English definitions of that label. As England supplied solutions to problems facing the empire, colonials rejected them as unacceptable. The more England pressed her answers upon the colonies, the more Americans questioned their ties to the empire.

America by 1763 had become a prosperous, fluid society, long past the stage of complete colonial dependency. The British did not understand this. They also failed to appreciate the tensions in

American society which they could have used to their own benefit. With the coming of peace with France in 1763, frontier farmers and Eastern landowners squared off for battle, urban mobs and wealthy merchants opposed one another, land speculators and settlers prepared for direct confrontation, and politicians concerted these rivalries into tools for their own purposes. Historian Carl Becker's famous dictum contains much truth: the American Revolution was a contest both for home rule and over who should rule at home. England's leaders failed to understand the divisiveness within American society. Instead, they pressed Americans and united them against a new set of common grievances, those emanating from London.

"The Young Band of Rebels"

The imperial upheaval, Professor Forrest McDonald has suggested, resulted in part from an identity crisis. America in the 1760's and 1770's was a nation of young people. Half the population was under sixteen, and three-quarters was under twenty-five. Its leaders, "a young band of rebels," came from this same age level. In 1776, James Monroe was eighteen, Alexander Hamilton and Rufus King were twenty-one, Gouverneur Morris was twenty-four, James Madison was twenty-six, Jefferson was thirty-three, and George Washington was an old man of forty-four. Three-eighths of the signers of the Constitution in 1787 were in their twenties and thirties. We often pay tribute to the brilliance of this generation, but we overlook its youthfulness.

This "romantic, lusty, and robust lot" led a revolution not only against imperial policies but against the imperial establishment in London. The outlook of these young colonials differed sharply from that of the older generation comfortably ensconced in Parliament and the Ministry. Americans challenged their parents' assumptions and those of imperial rulers because they found them narrow and restrictive. Young Americans had studied their Whig history well, and they used it to utmost advantage in confounding their elders.

Incident piled upon incident, giving Americans ample opportunity to respond and to define their positions more precisely. Beginning with the Sugar Act of 1764, the Stamp Act of 1765, the stationing of royal troops in the colonies, the Townshend Duties, the Tea Tax, the Boston Massacre, and finally the so-called Intolerable Acts, Americans pressed ever harder for a clear-cut definition of their place within the empire, a definition which the English had never offered and were unwilling to make at this time. England's unwillingness to accede to change, combined with young America's determination to force its acceptance, created the imperial crisis of 1776.

The Problem of Communication

Eighteenth-century communications are difficult for our world to appreciate. Accustomed to instant video relays, to round-the-world flights, to moon rockets, we find the delays inherent in sail transportation beyond our imagination. A normal eighteenth-century voyage between London and Boston, for example, took from five to six weeks. Should storms interfere, two or three more weeks might elapse between departure and arrival. This age knew little of navigational aids—Benjamin Franklin first guessed at the existence of the Gulf Stream and its impact upon transatlantic travel time.

Communication involved much more than transatlantic crossings, however. When a message from a colonial governor went to England, it had to pass from the point of debarkation into the hands of the appropriate official. This might take a week or ten days. Then the official cogitated about the matter, consulted his colleagues, secured approvals from the Board of Trade, the Attorney General, the Treasury Board, and the Secretary of War, heard representations from interested parties sometimes summoned from a distance, and finally won Privy Council approval for a proposed response. Such matters might well take months. Then and only then could an official answer make its tortuous return trip to the colony.

In sum, Anglo-American communications often required six

months from the inception of a query to the receipt of an answer. This had an impact all its own upon colonial government. Once a governor arrived in the New World, he was essentially on his own. He handled issues as they arose, hopefully using common sense with some political reality. Yet governors frequently found themselves bound and tied by intricate commissions and royal instructions. Controlled by men in London who had never visited the colonies, governors often found it necessary to transmit critical issues to imperial authorities for action.

Often, by the time official responses had been carefully developed in London, the problem had been settled in the colony, much to the dismay of imperial authorities and the governor on the scene. It was difficult to run a diversified empire covering so broad an expanse of territory given the nature of eighteenth-century communications. Indeed, one governor found his hands so thoroughly tied by his instructions that, upon learning the intentions of the colony's leaders and then reading his detailed instructions and understanding how little they coincided, he determined upon suicide as the only way out. Sir Danvers Osborne's governorship of New York lasted only long enough for him to understand the impossibility of his position.

Thus, when sharply defined crises arose in the 1760's and 1770's, colonial governors found themselves thrown on their own resources. Whether it involved opposition to the Stamp Act, violence as in the Boston Tea Party, or obstinacy when a legislature rejected the Mutiny Act and refused to vote supplies for royal troops, the governor knew that he alone must solve the problem— yet he must answer ultimately to London for his acts. To be a colonial governor in such strife-ridden times was an awesome task.

Differences of Societal Goals

A governor's life was further complicated by his obligation to transmit and translate an essentially English standard for American society. Yet the two peoples had different attitudes and goals. Americans, by virtue of their setting, emphasized a more adventuresome and speculative way of life than did the English, who seemed more tradition-bound. The New World environment became an important element in the drift that occurred between the two parts of the Anglo-American world.

Land ownership, for example, still held its lure as a status symbol and its immediate value as a means of livelihood. But in the New World land was plentiful and relatively easy to secure, whereas in the Old its acquisition was more often than not limited to an aristocracy of inherited or recently acquired wealth. In effect, this meant that the English viewed land ownership as a symbol of prestige and stability, qualities not always shared by the frontier landowner. English assumptions did not always coincide with American realities.

While England still thought, if not acted, in terms of a threefold division of society—King, Lords, and Commons—America really possessed but one of those three elements. The monarch, while held in veneration, was to colonists a distant and somewhat alien figure. The colonial aristocracy was one of talent rather than inheritance, and too familiar in local eyes to be venerated for its position alone. Local farmers remembered well when their squire was one of them, and their respect for his ability was often tinged with a bit of envy. America was a rude society on the make, with vast opportunities lying before it.

Western lands had always provided a sense of future for Americans. One sore point in Anglo-American relations centered on England's efforts to close off the colonists' major opportunity by the Proclamation Line of 1763 and later by the Quebec Act of 1774. The Proclamation Line, though intended as a temporary measure, threatened to close the West to immediate settlement. The Quebec Act, by regularizing settlement in an unacceptable way, did in fact close it. No colonist would enter a territory whose government did not include a legislative assembly, would live under the dreaded Roman Catholic Church, would exist under Roman rather than common law. What began as a palliative measure to satisfy the French Canadian population, to end squabbles among English colonies over control of the Western domain, and to provide a formal governmental structure to facilitate settlement—in other words, what began as a major positive innovation in British policy became proof to Americans of English perfidy, and they lumped the Quebec Act under the rubric "Intolerable Acts." More than anything else, England's intention with and America's reaction to the Quebec Act suggests the wide divergence between the societal goals of the two parts of the empire.

The Problem of Definitions

Until 1763 Americans gloried in their identification as Englishmen and proudly claimed all that the name implied. Fortunately for them and the empire, there was little need to define terms until 1763. Men on both sides of the Atlantic could talk of rights, representation, constitution, toleration, and similar ideals, and still disagree as to their meaning, for their disagreements never caused critical conflicts. There always seemed some politic way to avoid confrontation.

After 1763, as events moved rapidly, confrontation could no longer be avoided. England sought to reconstruct its empire, first by tightening up existing controls and, when that failed, by innovating new approaches. Each effort brought a response from American colonists that sharpened their definitions and simultaneously made them less comprehensible to Englishmen. English words acquired a different meaning on the Atlantic's western shore.

A prime example of this is the controversy over "representation." Americans had developed over the years a system of actual representation in local legislatures which differed notably from that used in England. The English system, which began as direct, actual representation, requiring the legislator to reside (or at least own property) in his district, had gradually become a system of virtual representation. Members of the House of Commons did not necessarily reside in their districts, and the view developed that members represented both districts and interests—that is, all farmers, merchants, artisans, and other occupations were represented in Parliament if only one of them, or one member representing a group of them, sat in Commons.

The English finally formalized this arrangement by repealing the residency requirement, but Americans moved in precisely the opposite direction. As early as the 1690's Massachusetts passed a residency requirement for its General Court. New York in the 1760's refused seats to several legislators who did not reside in districts they represented. And other colonies followed the same pattern.

Thus the outcome of the controversy between England and her colonies over virtual representation proved predictable. When Parliament claimed the right to tax Americans, who as Englishmen were *virtually* represented in the House of Commons, colonists could not believe their ears. So determined were Americans on this point that they eventually wrote specific residence requirements into state constitutions and the federal constitution. (In recent years we have moved slightly away from this restriction, though the laws themselves have not changed.)

American concepts of constitutionalism also differed sharply from those held by Englishmen. To colonials a constitution was a written contractual arrangement, while to Englishmen it was a flexible pattern of government. In looking at the English constitution, Americans saw a fixed charter of government, unalterable by any of its parts. Such rigidity was absurd in the light of British governmental practices, but Americans had built this concept over three-quarters of a century and would not deviate from it.

Similarly, they looked upon their own local governmental arrangements as fixed contractual forms. Colonies fortunate enough to have royal charters considered them inflexible and absolute protections against royal interference. Colonies without charters converted precedent, Magna Carta, and the Bill of Rights of 1688 into fixed and rigid constitutions. And they looked upon the governor's commission as a limiting document rather than one which offered him an opportunity to innovate.

Such restrictions were unknown in England. Under a parliamentary form of government without written limits, only a sense of propriety restricted public authority. Blackstone, famous compiler and annotator of the common law, once noted that Parliament had power to do anything but turn a man into a woman. (Now, even that limitation has seemingly been cast aside.) As the English pressured the colonials, Americans reaffirmed their belief in finite limits upon governmental power, an idea that had no meaning whatever for Englishmen. No one in England understood colonials when they insisted that a parliamentary statute was unconstitutional. Failure to impose their definitions upon the mother country led Americans eventually to abandon the "rights of Englishmen" for "natural rights," on the assumption that in joining society men gave up only certain powers and retained all others indefinitely and without limit. This was the rationale behind the Declaration of Independence.

The Experience of Self-government

Still another factor with which the English contended after 1763 was America's long-demonstrated ability to govern itself. From the Glorious Revolution of 1688 to the end of the French and Indian War in 1763, colonists evolved patterns of local government well suited to their needs. The power of assemblies constantly expanded at the expense of royal and proprietary governors' authority, often despite ineffectual English protests.

The key to the rise of colonial assemblies was their power over finances. On innumerable occasions, English authorities were urged to establish a "civil list," a fund from the English Exchequer for payment of royal officials in the colonies. This would eliminate their dependence on assemblies and make them truly capable of carrying out English policy. But Parliament remained shortsighted and never willingly burdened the English taxpayer with the costs of empire, even though England derived important benefits from its overseas possessions.

Lack of a civil list placed the burden of supporting royal

officials—governors, justices, councillors, and others—squarely on local assemblies. And these bodies looked back to English practices and copied them with deftness. Legislative control of finances often began, as it had in Elizabeth I's England, with an insistence that grievances must first be answered before supplies were voted. From that first demand, colonial assemblies proceeded to determine the proper use for their funds. When they met with obstructive tactics from royal governors, assemblies not only introduced line-item budgets but appointed their own treasurers whose signatures were necessary on warrants for the issuance of money.

Such tactics were fought by governors and by English authorities, but no assembly could be coerced into raising taxes, and most had wisely refrained from granting funds on a long-term basis. England's alternatives, then, were to accept money on the assembly's terms, to have the British Exchequer pay for the colony's upkeep, or to allow the government to go without funds. Since the last two were unthinkable, imperial authorities gave in, though not always gracefully.

So pervasive did assembly control become that royal governors could no longer look to their councils for support in preserving royal authority. The local political structure became so intricate that councillors, rather than representing the King's authority, became leaders of factional alignments tied closely to the assembly. Thus governors, instead of working with a group of loyal advisers, found themselves arguing with leaders of the opposition, especially when local interests collided with imperial ones.

Readers of Whig Textbooks

In their contests with royal officials, colonials utilized the vast radical literature that emerged in England during the eighteenth century. This material, written by those whom Professor Caroline Robbins has dubbed the "Eighteenth-Century Commonwealthmen," gave Americans, especially after 1763, excellent theoretical ammunition. It offered an idea of government acceptable to colonials and verified by their experiences.

On the basis of this radical literature, their own experiences, and the writings of John Locke, Americans conceived of constitutions as contractual arrangements, written and fixed, to be ended only when one party irremediably violated the agreement. Locke's role in this development of American ideas was most important. Colonials meticulously examined his writings and refined his concepts to apply them to their needs. Before 1776 they never carried through with his theory of justifiable revolution, but in that year they accepted his ideas on that point as well.

Americans avidly read of seventeenth- and early eighteenth-century English parliamentary development, and they adapted those aspects that seemed to fit their own needs. Every assembly mimicked the House of Commons in all possible ways. In presenting its speaker to the governor, an assembly copied the Commons presentation of its speaker to the King, and requested the same rights. Almost every privilege won by Commons in the seventeenth century could be found duplicated in eighteenth-century colonial legislatures, and assemblies fought every attempt by a royal governor to abridge those privileges.

As avid readers of English history, Americans gloried in the expansion of English liberties and identified with the progressive improvement of man's condition. Enlightenment ideas current in the eighteenth century reinforced American prejudices. Americans read Montesquieu (not republished in America until 1802) in imported editions, as well as Burlamaqui, Rousseau, and other literary notables of the eighteenth century.

The Paranoid Nature of American Politics

Combined with problems of communication, differences in societal goals, variations in definitions of terms, American experience in self-government, and the pervasive Whig orientation of the period was a basic Anglo-American political attitude. Politics on both sides of the Atlantic suffered from a popular paranoia.

Americans in particular tended under pressure to extend their arguments to logical extremes, and then to assume that those extremes were the intended goals. Americans came by this phenomenon honestly enough, having brought it with them as part of their cultural baggage from England, but they made more effective use of it than their British cousins. Americans dreaded conspiracies and found them everywhere they looked. If conspiracies did not actually exist, Americans invented them. This helps explain American popular reactions to imperial policy in the 1760's and 1770's.

A reading of contemporary American newspapers, pamphlets, and tracts immediately suggests that British intentions went far beyond the raising of £60,000 by means of a stamp duty. Lurking deep within British breasts, colonials thought, was clearly a scheme to transfer all or almost all of their debt burden to Americans, and the stamp duty was but the first step. Time and time again this theme was repeated by colonists arguing against British policies. If they acceded to one tax, they gave away the whole game, because then they could no longer contend against the principle of taxation.

This habit of reading ulterior motives into the actions of others certainly worked effectively for American propagandists who stirred up colonial opposition to British policy. They touched a delicate nerve and built up a mass hysteria by the time of the Declaration of Independence. Passage of the Quebec Act in 1774, for example, seemed the beginning of a plot to impose Roman Catholicism upon all the colonies, to strip them of their legislative assemblies, and to deny them all rights under English common law. Nothing was further from the minds of responsible English officials, but an irrational argument cannot be answered rationally.

Much of what happened between 1763 and 1776 came as a consequence of mass paranoia in America. Had the colonists accepted or rejected English policy strictly on its merits, there would have been no revolt in 1776, for British policy, viewed rationally, seemed too unimportant to disrupt the ancient Anglo-American connection. Yet, when interpreted in the guise of a plot to undermine and destroy American liberties, British policy became ominous and foreboding.

The theme of plot and counterplot runs through American history to the present day. One need only consider the Federalist reaction which culminated in the Alien and Sedition Acts, the nativist response to immigration in the period from 1830 to 1850, the Southern attitude toward geographical limitation of slavery in the 1850's, the agrarian response to big business in the 1890's, and Senator Joseph McCarthy's witchhunt in the 1950's to realize that this is an ancient and indelible—though sometimes dishonorable—tradition in American life.

Consequences of Rebellion

Americans rebelled in 1776 against an imperial system which seemed to them corrupt and intolerable. Yet it had given them protection against powerful enemies, nurtured them into economic maturity, and provided them with greater liberty than that enjoyed by any other colonial population. Americans understood the benefits of central authority, but they insisted on its purity and rejected it only when it became intolerably corrupt.

Identification with central authority remained an American trait even during the Revolution. The moment of rebellion itself was created by a new American central authority which supplanted the empire. Individual states did not declare independence; rather, the thirteen states assembled as the Second Continental Congress repudiated British authority. The Congress then assumed all the functions of central government except for the sensitive areas of taxation and the regulation of commerce.

Though an *ad hoc* arrangement, the Congress continued in existence until 1781, coordinating the war effort, conducting foreign relations, and generally making the rebellion effective. Its lengthy existence had not been intended. When Richard Henry Lee introduced his resolution for independence on June 7, 1776, he also called for international alliances and the creation of a permanent central government. Thus Americans not only broke their ties with the empire by means of a central agency, but they simultaneously proposed creation of a new central government.

In structuring their new government, Americans imposed safeguards to prevent future perversions of its power. They believed, in traditional eighteenth-century terms, that all power inhered in the people who, when they formed a government, delegated to it certain powers and reserved the balance to themselves. Thus to prevent future abuses they retained for themselves and denied to the central government those powers they had found to be capable of abuse, specifically taxation and regulation of commerce. The new Articles of Confederation proved a mirror image, not of what the British Empire had been but of what Americans believed it *should* have been. It had all the authority necessary and proper for the functions assigned to it, but none of those which had led the empire into difficulties. Once Virginia ceded its Western land claims to the Articles government in 1781, Maryland consented to the Articles and the new government became operative.

Under the Articles the nation made significant progress in some areas. Rules for disposing of Western lands were adopted in 1784 and revised a year later, and a system of territorial government was established in 1787 (the Northwest Ordinance). In formulating this measure, Americans resolved a basic issue on which the empire had foundered: America would have no permanent colonies but would follow a clear-cut, nonpolitical procedure for converting territories (or colonies) into states fully equal with the original thirteen. The Articles government also adjusted boundary disputes, operated a postal system, signed treaties with foreign nations, controlled Indian affairs, and developed an administrative structure.

But the Articles government suffered from its inability to tax or to regulate commerce. It could not repay its debts, domestic and foreign, raise funds for current expenses, retaliate against trade discrimination by other nations, or curb interstate trade and tariff rivalries among its own members. Each attempt to overcome these deficiencies met with failure, and an ensuing sense of frustration led to a campaign for a complete overhaul of the frame of government.

Perhaps the greatest weapon given to those seeking radical changes and a stronger central government was the abortive rebellion in Massachusetts in 1786 led by Daniel Shays. Again America's paranoid tendency appeared as proponents of a stronger central government exaggerated the rebellion's seriousness. The failure of the Articles government to protect its own arsenal at Springfield, coupled with fears of similar rebellions elsewhere, spurred many seriously to consider revamping the Articles.

After several tentative moves toward revision of the Articles, a convention finally assembled at Philadelphia in 1787. Though called to revise the Articles, the convention quickly agreed to abandon that covenant and create a new one. The gathering met in secret to avoid embarrassment or worse, for its members were actually planning a *coup d'état* and finally produced the federal Constitution. The document was transmitted to the Articles of Confederation Congress with a request that it be sent to the states for ratification.

Some claim that the Constitution represented a counterrevolutionary movement; others insist that it was the logical culmination of the Revolution. Both viewpoints can be argued with some success. Certainly the best-known firebrands of the Revolution did not participate in the convention and refused to support the finished product. Patrick Henry and Sam Adams did not attend, and Thomas Jefferson, who was in France on official business, wrote back critically about the Constitution. Yet many of those at the Philadelphia convention had been in the forefront of the Revolution: Washington, Franklin, and Madison were as notorious by their presence as the others were by their absence. Alexander Hamilton, one of this generation's brilliant young men, participated in the debates, reluctantly signed the Constitution as too weak but the best obtainable, and vigorously defended the convention's results in the *Federalist Papers,* with Madison and John Jay.

But none of its supporters regarded the Constitution as a final and finished product. No governmental charter was viewed as immutable, as a "sacred cow." The very fact that the Constitution was the second frame and the third government established within a decade suggested that this generation was not averse to experimentation. Jefferson was perfectly honest when he suggested that no one generation had any right to bind future generations, that each age should periodically review the actions of its predecessor.

Those assembled at Philadelphia realized that they had not offered a final pronouncement on governmental organization. Indeed, they found themselves disagreeing on many points and so left them vague. By slurring over their own disagreements, they left it to future generations to fill in many details of governmental structure. This was perhaps the Founding Fathers' greatest gift, for it permitted a government constructed for an agrarian society to adapt with only slight modification to the world's most highly industrialized and urbanized nation.

The framers readily understood the Constitution's imperfection and impermanence. Its opponents immediately denounced the omission of a Bill of Rights. This argument provided an opportunity for the Constitution's proponents to co-opt their antagonists by promising to remedy the oversight as soon as the new government became effective. Under the guidance of James Madison, a series of proposals were reduced to twelve amendments which passed the new Congress and went to the states for ratification. Ten of these were finally adopted and became the Bill of Rights.

When George Washington took office as President under the federal Constitution, the American people had come full cycle. They had overthrown one empire only to replace it with a new one. The primary difference between the two was the locus of power. In the British empire, ultimate authority rested three thousand miles away in London, and the governed had no means of controlling their governors. In the new system, authority rested within the society. The Founding Fathers, despite their lack of faith in the people, had so arranged matters that more and more power over governors could gradually pass into the hands of the governed. It was their greatest contribution to the science of government.

A Brief Chronology of the Revolution

1770	March 5	Boston Massacre
	March 12	Townshend Duties repealed except for tax on tea
1773	May 10	Parliament passes Tea Act giving East India Company monopoly of American tea market
	December 16	Boston Tea Party
1774	March 31–May 20	Coercive or "Intolerable" Acts passed by Parliament
	September 5	First Continental Congress meets in Philadelphia
1775	April 19	Battles of Lexington and Concord
	May 2	Second Continental Congress meets in Philadelphia
	June 17	Battle of Bunker Hill
	August–December	Americans try to liberate Canada but are repulsed
1776	January 1	Lord Dunmore burns Norfolk, Virginia
	January 15	Thomas Paine's *Common Sense* published
	March 17	England evacuates Boston
	June 7	Richard Henry Lee introduces resolution in Congress for independence
	July 2	Congress adopts Declaration of Independence
	September 15	British occupy New York City
1777	October 17	Burgoyne's army surrenders at Saratoga
1778	February 6	Franco-American alliance signed
1781	October 19	Cornwallis surrenders at Yorktown
1782	March 20	Lord North's ministry falls
	November 30	Preliminary Articles of Peace signed

1784	April 23	Jefferson's land ordinance adopted by Confederation Congress
1786	January 16	Virginia adopts Jefferson's Statute for Religious Freedom
	September 11–14	Annapolis Convention meets
	August–December	Shays' Rebellion in Massachusetts
1787	May 25	Constitutional Convention opens in Philadelphia
	July 13	Northwest Ordinance passed by Confederation Congress
	September 17	Constitution receives final approval at convention
	December 7	Delaware is first to ratify Constitution
1788	June 21	New Hampshire is ninth state to ratify Constitution
1789	January 7	First presidential election chooses Washington and Adams
	September 9–25	First ten amendments to Constitution approved by Congress and submitted to states
1791	December 15	Bill of Rights becomes part of Constitution

Part 1

THE REVOLUTIONARY GENERATION

SINCE THE days of Thomas Carlyle, if not earlier, historians have debated the conundrum of whether men make history or history makes men. As a philosophical exercise the question has some merits; as a practical matter it has less significance. The American Revolution is especially subject to such debate because it brought together a critical configuration of men and events. In terms of political history it produced at an auspicious moment a brilliant generation of leaders, sometimes referred to as America's "golden age."

In thinking of the Revolutionary generation, one young man is frequently overlooked, and certainly oversimplified. Historians usually have dealt with King George III as either a fool or a knave, largely as a consequence of his "bad press" at the hands of such superb propagandists as Thomas Paine and Thomas Jefferson. Americans needed a scapegoat for their unhappiness with the empire, and George III fit the bill. The colonists had destroyed their ties of affection with all English institutions save the monarchy by 1776; only veneration of the King bound them to Britain. Both Paine and Jefferson realized that until Americans severed that bond, they could not declare their independence. Paine disabused the colonists of their idealization of monarchy as an institution, while Jefferson destroyed their regard for the reigning monarch. From this double-barreled assault, George III's reputation suffered mightily.

Only recently have historians viewed George III as a victim of a system over which he had little control. By plumbing the intricacies of eighteenth-century English politics, scholars, led by Sir Lewis Namier, have given new insight into George III. Rather than an evil genius, the King now appears a simple man, often inadequate to the great demands made on him by his times. In the first article to follow, the English historian A. L. Rowse summarizes recent reinterpretations of George III and concludes that he was a latter-day King Canute who sought to hold back the waves of time.

Opposing the King's efforts to maintain the unity of his empire was a brilliant array of colonial theorists and activists. The oldest of them, who brought to the Revolution vast experience in public office, was Benjamin Franklin, referred to by Henry Steele Commager as "an intruder into posterity." Franklin's career spanned the eighteenth century and reflected many of the changes of his times. At age seventy-three, when most men slip contentedly into retirement, he began his greatest role as a revolutionary.

Another old man of the Revolution was George Washington. By all ordinary criteria he should have been a Tory: he had the wealth, position, experience, and age necessary to keep him loyal to the Crown. Instead he became a conservative revolutionary, a moderate leader of young rebels. Beginning with the famed Parson Weems, a legend developed around Washington which has stripped him of his warmth and personality. This device has served Americans as a response to their own needs, but it has served Washington poorly. A school of "debunkers" has rescued the General by emphasizing his foibles. John A. Krout suggests that Washington's humanity can be uncovered by realizing that his accomplishments were those of a simple man. Krout condemns both extremes of deification and degradation for the mistaken portrait they offer of an important Revolutionary figure. Seelye Jones compares Washington to his contemporaries and to more modern leaders.

American veneration of Revolutionary leaders extends also to Thomas Jefferson, but with strikingly different results. Jefferson, a man of diverse talents enmeshed in partisan politics for many years, has never been obscured by false idolization. Best known for his ideas rather than his actions—indeed, this was his wish for his epitaph—he has become one of the most appealing figures of the era. Each generation has used Jeffersonian principles to justify its own actions. Allan Nevins suggests that Jefferson was "our most eloquent apostle of democracy," and that in itself has served to keep his memory fresh. Jefferson the man of action is neglected; Jefferson the philosopher has been found useful by men of all political convictions. Indeed, as Saul Padover notes, Jefferson's ideological contributions transcend America's borders and give him an international dimension.

Not all of our Revolutionary leaders have been apotheosized. Alexander Hamilton's reputation has dimmed over the years, perhaps because those espousing ultra-conservative causes have seized upon him as their symbol. As Dorothie Bobbe suggests, the Hamiltonian myths are not easily stripped away because of this false image which others have created. Hamilton possessed every ingredient necessary to become a popular hero—youth, brilliance, brashness, and flamboyance. Even his early death in a duel with Aaron Burr (certainly no hero in anyone's book) should have secured his position as an American idol, but such has not been his fate.

One problem of the Revolution was a confusion of loyalties. The Revolution both repelled and attracted individuals. A number of Europeans came to America's aid, some for idealistic reasons and some to make their reputations and fortunes. A good illustration of the idealistic individual who brought important talents to the American cause was Baron von Steuben. H. I. Brock discusses his role as typical of the help Washington received from such mercenaries. On the other hand, Benedict Arnold represents the classic tragedy of the Revolution—those whose faith was too frail to permit their continued support of the Revolution. Randolph G. Adams discusses Arnold's career on the basis of the Clinton, or Headquarters, Papers of the British army.

Finally, one essay brings us back to the essential point: this was an age of giants. The luminaries thus far discussed were merely representative of their generation, and others who participated with as much importance are frequently overlooked. Dumas Malone assesses the love of liberty and the courage to risk all in its behalf as the touchstone of this generation.

New and Kind Light on George III

by A. L. Rowse

ON OCT. 25, 1760, George III succeeded to the throne, a somewhat underdeveloped young man of twenty-two. His long reign of sixty years was in some ways the apogee of English history, though it witnessed the cataclysm of the American Revolution. That resounding event, or rather series of events, we must regard —looking at it from the point of view of its illimitable significance for the future—as the most important in the whole eighteenth century, even more important than the French Revolution.

Indeed, its significance for the world is only equaled by that of the Russian Revolution in our time. We might justly regard the main conflict raging in the world today as one between the ideals of the American Revolution and those of the Russian. For American ideals had, and have, a revolutionary appeal no less than Communist dogmas, even if their appeal is altogether more humane and civilized, offering far more hope to mankind than the sinister denial of freedom from which the brutality and barbarity of communism flow. As between Washington and Jefferson on one side, and Lenin and Stalin on the other, who can hesitate?

Where does King George III come into this?

I think we can properly, if somewhat popularly, regard him as a kind of King Canute attempting to hold up the advance of the waves. We can hardly blame him, for, being a man of limited capacity, he certainly did not understand the profounder movements out in the ocean that produced such tremendous tides.

Historians now recognize that George III was a much maligned man, both in his own day and subsequently in the writing of history. It so happened that his opponents, the Whigs, had all the best writers; they had not only most of the men of genius but the future with them, and they fixed the legend of George as a corrupt tyrant, acting unconstitutionally, engaged in a conspiracy against English liberties. None of this is true.

The Whig historians, though brilliant writers, were not very perceptive psychologists. With our knowledge of psychology, we can easily see that George III offers a clear psychotic case. He was a retarded youth, lethargic and rather stupid; he had been brought up piously by his mother, the widowed Princess of Wales, in great innocence of the world which, she thought (quite rightly in the fashionable world of the eighteenth century), would corrupt his morals. As a young man he had an utter lack of confidence in himself, which is rather touching—and yet there was this great station coming to him which he felt himself quite unable to fill.

"My Dearest Friend," he wrote to his mentor, Lord Bute, "I am deeply afflicted at the many things you told me. They have set me in a most dreadful light before my own eyes. I now see plainly that I have been my greatest enemy; for had I always acted according to your advice, I should now have been the direct opposite from what I am; nothing but the true love you bear me, could have led you to remain with me so long, or to speak to me in the manner you have of late."

To set against this lack of confidence and his natural indolence, the young King had only one asset: that absolute devotion to duty which was the strongest suit in the Hanoverian royal house, and which enabled the Hanoverians to survive when the native Stuarts went down. There was indeed a German quality about it, as there was about all George III's characteristics. For we must remember that George III, like his predecessors, George I and George II, and his successors, were German by blood; he had hardly a drop of English blood in him.

For the sake of duty he sacrificed his proper inclinations: he had fallen in love with the enchanting Lady Sarah Lennox, but he was not allowed to marry an Englishwoman. So he married Queen Charlotte and lived with her happily enough; with her he usually talked German.

The quality of his addiction to duty was quite un-English; he made himself a martyr to duty, a martinet to those about him. He could not bear the slapdash amateurishness of the English aristocrats, who thought themselves qualified to take on anything they had a mind to, whether trained to it or not. Nor was the King wholly wrong. Can one altogether blame him for disliking the thought of placing the Treasury in the hands of Charles James Fox, who had gambled an immense fortune away and lived in perpetual debt?

Eighteenth-century aristocrats took all this lightheartedly enough; not so the King, who was more *ernst* and more emotional. There is no evidence that he had any sense of humor to help him, either; they had plenty, perhaps too much for good sense, and they found him and his dull, plain German wife very funny.

Economical, respectable "Farmer George" was never popular either with London fashionable society or the London mob. His tastes were in keeping: simple fare, boiled mutton and turnips, constant open-air exercise, mechanical contrivances which made them ridicule him as "the royal button-maker."

He had the German taste for experts and military detail; among the arts he liked music best, Handel being his favorite composer. He was responsible for the successful career of the astronomer Herschel in England, and had an addiction to astronomy. Ill-educated, he was curious about everything and forever was asking everybody quick-fire questions, ending with "What? What?" When he was recovering from one of his attacks of insanity, Horace Walpole called his conversation "coming back to his nonsense."

Of course, the strain the King put upon himself, in addition to the incessant wear of politics, crises, war and family troubles, brought about periodic breakdowns. Trying to live up to his overwhelming sense of duty as King, he strained himself to reach unattainable standards—for he was, after all, not a remarkable man but only a man of ordinary capacities.

He did succeed in turning himself into a very hard worker, though there was an element of the psychotic in this: he was forever fussing, interfering, could not let well enough alone— all the signs of an anxiety complex.

His most displeasing characteristic was a hard strain of implacability. Although there was a genuine kindness in him, a constant wish to do good and a generosity in his charities, he was less generous to people, of whom he was censorious.

This being, as I see it, the character of the King, what was his attitude to the earthquake that opened under his feet with the American Revolution?

It was very much what one would expect from such a person in such a position.

Looking back over it all, it is clear that the American Revolution was inevitable. And though historians have gone on arguing about it ever since, placing the emphasis or the blame here or there, the essence of the matter seems to me as simple as the question Tom Paine put with such effect at the time: "To know whether it be the interest of this continent to be independent, we need only ask this easy, simple question: Is it the interest of a man to be a boy all his life?"

The colonies had grown up to maturity faster and more completely than anyone, perhaps even they themselves, realized. For here is a consideration that I have not seen expressed elsewhere: when one considers the rapidity with which a great new state organized itself, forged all its instruments, created its forms, came to the fore in one bound with a marvelous galaxy of ability and talent such as has not since been surpassed—there is nothing like a revolution as a forced pump for ability—it is evident that America was ripe, indeed over-ripe, for self-government.

Historians would agree, I think, that the King was not to blame for the measures that provoked and brought on the Revolution, stupid and ill-considered as they were—such measures as the Stamp Act, the Declaratory Act, the Townshend Duties and Lord North's dumping of tea. George Grenville, the competent, unimaginative administrator—a Neville Chamberlain of his time —who started government on this regressive course was personally a man the King could not abide. "I would rather see the devil in my closet than George Grenville," he said. "When he has wearied me for two hours, he looks at his watch to see if he may not tire me for one hour more."

The King gladly got rid of Grenville, was not opposed to the repeal of the Stamp Act and, in regard to the resistance of Boston, expressed his "desire with temper to let them return to their reason, not with violence to drive them."

But the fundamental issue of sovereignty was insoluble in eighteenth-century terms and on this issue the King was at one with the great bulk of politically conscious opinion in Britain; there could be only one sovereignty and there was no doubt where constitutionally it lay.

Only a very original mind such as Franklin's could argue, "from a long and thorough consideration of the subject," that the Empire was not a single state, but several; that "the Parliament has no right to make any law whatever, binding on the colonies * * * the King, and not the King, Lords and Commons collectively, is their sovereign * * * the King, with their respective Parliaments, is their only legislator." More briefly, Franklin argued, "their only bond of union is the King."

It was not until the twentieth century that Franklin's concept of dominion status could be realized. No one in England in the eighteenth century could grasp such an idea, except a very small minority of radicals and dissenters on the extreme left; and it certainly may be doubted whether it could have been given practical effect.

The King himself would have had the greatest objection to it: he would have considered it contrary to his duty as a parliamentary monarch. He once described himself as "an old Whig," which he was: for him alone to accept sovereignty of America—to become King of America—apart from the British Parliament, would have seemed to him an invitation to become an irresponsible despot. Anyway, the idea was not, in those days, practical politics; if he had accepted such a thing, he would have been turned off the throne.

Though we must blame the Government rather than the King for provoking the Revolution, we can justly blame him for prolonging it, for keeping poor Lord North, who never had believed in the war, at it year after year. This was where George III's obtuse, psychotic obstinacy came in—obtuse because it *was* psychotic.

We know why the King kept the war up year after year, when he should have given in: he left records of what he thought about American independence in acres of papers. He was absolutely convinced, and frequently so stated, that the dissolution of the union would be the destruction of his country.

What he meant by "destruction" we also know from his letters: he meant that, without America, Britain would be relegated to the position of a second-rate power in Europe. He could not bear the idea of presiding over such a dissolution, to use Churchill's phrase to Roosevelt over India in our time. So he plodded on and on, in his Germanic fashion, after others in England had seen the game was up and were ready to accept the inevitable.

The extraordinary thing was that, when the English woke up from the shock of the catastrophe, they found that the destruction many had fully expected had not taken place. Britain picked herself up and went forward—to find herself in a few years doing a more prosperous trade with the independent United States than ever before with the recalcitrant colonies. And, as the nineteenth century progressed and free trade continued, the immense prosperity of Britain went along with, and was largely due to, the expansion of America.

Thus are people's worst fears sometimes belied by experience.

Franklin Still Speaks to Us

by Henry Steele Commager

"I SEEM to have intruded myself into the company of posterity," wrote the aged Benjamin Franklin at the Constitutional Convention of 1787. And his observation was prophetic, for the one company in which we can be sure to find Dr. Franklin is the company of posterity.

What the dying John Adams said of Thomas Jefferson is even more true of Franklin, that he "still survives." He has survived in countless ways and places—in the school readers studied by millions of boys and girls in each generation, in a thousand names over the land, in the thrust of engines driven by dynamos, and the thrust of power of the great republic he helped to found, in the religion of good works and the zeal for private associations, in the philosophy of pragmatism and the principles and practices of service, in the spirit that animates the best of our newspapers, and the best of our diplomats, in the language spoken by tens of millions of Americans, in history and mythology, in the imagination of Americans and in their hearts.

He is the most contemporary of the Founding Fathers, the

only one, we feel, who would get along famously in the America of our own day. Yet he is, too, much the oldest of the Founding Fathers. He was an active young man when Cotton Mather was unraveling Puritan theology and John Wise writing his Vindication and William Byrd of Virginia his secret diary; he was an active old man when Henry Clay and Daniel Webster and John C. Calhoun were disporting themselves innocently in a world still in the making. Franklin links the world of Locke and Newton to the world of Clay's American system, of Lincoln's homely aphorisms and William James' pragmatism.

"A great man," wrote Justice Holmes, "represents a strategic point in the campaign of history, and a part of his greatness consists in his being *there*." Franklin was most certainly *there:* there at the Albany Congress, there in Carpenter's Hall to help with the Declaration of Independence, there with the committee that drew up the articles of Union, there at the peace negotiations that acknowledged American independence, and there in the Convention that prepared the Constitution of the United States. He was ubiquitous, he was persuasive. He was there in England— for sixteen years—and in France for another nine; he was the most traveled American, the most cosmopolitan.

He was *there,* too, in a spiritual sense, and still is. Wherever you turned in Philadelphia, there was Franklin: in the academy that became the university, in the hospital, in the Philosophical Society, in the Society Library; the very streets were paved by Franklin, lighted by Franklin, cleaned by Franklin, protected by Franklin, and every house with its Franklin stove and its lightning rod proclaimed his presence!

And what was the strategic point in history? It was the emergence in the world of a new nation, a new society, a new economy, perhaps even a new culture. It was that experiment which Jefferson called "the world's best hope" and in which, said Washington, "the destiny of unborn Millions was involved." If we may imagine the "campaign" of history to be one for the mitigation of the ravages of nationalism, for the ending of colonialism, for the triumph of self-government, for the spread of material well-being, for progress of social equality, for the advancement of learning and science, then the American experience is indeed a strategic point in that campaign. And then Franklin represents better perhaps than any other man of his time that strategic point.

No other American, except Jefferson, touched American life on so many sides, or left so lasting an impress from his touch. Journalist, scientist, politician, diplomat, educator, administrator, writer, philosopher, he was a universal genius, but the most modest and most moderate of geniuses. It was, to be sure, an age of versatility, when kings played flutes and statesmen wrote dramas and jurists spouted poetry and physicists indulged in theology. And in America versatility was, perhaps, exaggerated, for there even theologians and statesmen had to know how to plant potatoes and saw wood and doctor a slave or an apprentice.

But even in the eighteenth century, and even in America, Franklin was phenomenal; he could contrive, with equal facility, a plan for a subscription library or colonial union; he could fashion a new stove or a new commonwealth; he could organize a fire company, a post office, or an international alliance; he could invent a new musical instrument, test the winds and the tides, chart the Gulf Stream, and confound mathematicians with magical squares. He could snatch the lightning from heaven and the scepter from tyrants. He was a sort of historical Robinson Crusoe, prepared to new-make everything, inventive, ingenious, resourceful, competent, symbol of a society of Robinson Crusoes.

It is perhaps the unfailing competence that is most impressive. Whatever Franklin did, he did well, and with what seemed effortless ease, from the establishment of his newspapers to the complicated peace negotiations with Vergennes and Oswald. How simple the electrical experiments seem to us—they are reduced to flying a kite so even little children can seem to understand and enjoy them—and how profound were the scientific laws that emerged from the experiments! How effortless the prose of the Autobiography, tossed off for the pleasure of a son, and how difficult to imitate and impossible to match! How familiar the sayings of Poor Richard, and how awkward to be called upon to

make up others as effective! There was genius in the famous
epitaph—composed when Franklin was but 22—but it was the
genius of simplicity:

The Body of
B. Franklin Printer,
(Like the Cover of an old Book
Its Contents torn out
And Stript of its Lettering & Gilding)
Lies here, Food for Worms.
But the Work shall not be lost;
For it will (as he believ'd) appear
once more
In a new and more elegant Edition
Revised and corrected
By the Author.

Franklin was a child of the Age of Reason, and it is reasonableness that characterizes all his interests and his conduct. He had
a tidy mind, and hated to see things go to waste—time, energy,
resources. He was prepared to let well enough alone (as with the
finished Constitution), but rarely found anything that really
seemed well enough. His zeal for improvements was a product
of a sense of duty rather than of fanaticism, and he was the most
amiable of all reformers.

He was reasonable with his business rivals and usually joined
them or bought them out; he was reasonable with the misguided
Members of Parliament who did not understand the American
position. He was reasonable with Jefferson about changes in the
Declaration, and reasonable with himself about defects in the
Constitution.

He saw no reason why his beloved Philadelphia should not be
cleaned up and organized, and he saw no real reason why humanity at large should not, similarly, be tidied up and organized along
sensible lines. But he was the least doctrinaire of men, and
would never impose his own schemes or theories upon others.

The versatility, the competence, the reasonableness, the compromise, these are qualities we associate with what was to be American, and one reason that Americans came to cherish these qualities is that Franklin made them so attractive. America was to be many things, and Franklin represented most of them.

"It seems I am too much of an American," he said to an English friend when he prepared to return to Pennsylvania after many years in the Mother Country, and he reflected, not unhappily, that "old trees cannot be safely transplanted." He enjoyed his life abroad, but he was never really transplanted; he took his America with him wherever he went.

He was American in his democracy, not merely in political principles but in social practices. He was the spokesman for all apprentices who ran away, for all the printers who dared criticize their betters or challenge the impudence of government, for all colonials who wondered how the Toms, Dicks and Harriets of London could "hoist themselves onto the throne of the King and talk of Our Colonies in America."

He was the boy who made good, the outsider who crashed all the gates of Philadelphia, the American who had stood before five kings "and had the honor of sitting down to dinner with one"; the diplomat clad in homespun who had outwitted the diplomats of the Old World.

But he was a democrat by conviction as well as by instinct. He was largely responsible for the unicameral legislature in Pennsylvania, and recommended it for the new United States. In the Constitutional Convention he spoke up for democracy. "Doctor Franklin," so Madison reports, "expressed his dislike of everything that tended to debase the spirit of the common people."

He was a nationalist, too, in the sense that he saw the thirteen colonies as part of the single whole. As Postmaster General he had visited every colony and he early came to think in American terms; perhaps the fact that he himself came from Massachusetts Bay and that Pennsylvania was the most heterogeneous of colonies contributed to his point of view.

He started newspapers in Massachusetts, New York, New Jersey and South Carolina; he came to be agent in London for half a dozen colonies. He had no fear of Union or of a strong central government, and thought disobedience in the states more dangerous than despotism in the nation.

His most important contribution has been neglected, in part because he made so little of it himself. That was the contribution to federalism, one of the great inventions of the new nation. He had drawn up the Albany Plan of Union back in 1754; he served on the committee that drafted the Articles of Confederation in the Seventeen Seventies; he was one of the presiding elders in the Convention that gave us our present Constitution. Thus he had seen the nature of the problem of imperial organization back in the Fifties; he celebrated the solution of the problem over thirty years later. Alone of the Founding Fathers, he provides continuity and unity to this achievement.

But it is in the homelier virtues, or perhaps the more private, that Franklin seems to have anticipated so much of the America of the future.

There was, for example, his passion for self-improvement—self-improvement by no means for purely material reasons; he is the godfather of a thousand adult education programs. There is his zeal to do good; everyone is familiar with the story in the Autobiography that tells how he "made a little book" and kept account of progress in morals; it should be remembered that the "precept of Order" posed each morning the question, "What good shall I do this day?" and each night the question, "What good have I done to-day?"

All his life Franklin was a practical philanthropist, and he may be said to have set the example that America has followed more affluently than has any other country. There is that practical idealism—a trait so hard for outsiders to understand—that enabled him to combine deism with support to orthodox churches, provide complicated arrangements for self-help to apprentices and Free Negroes, and arrange for fire companies and police protection through taxation.

It is, indeed, fatally easy to exaggerate the purely practical side of Franklin, to make of him the first Rotarian, and we have tended to overemphasize this. It should be remembered that Franklin retired at 42—when he had a modest competence—to find time for scientific research and for study; that he devoted the next forty years of his life to science and learning, and to ill-paid public duty; that he gave incessantly of himself and his money to public causes; that he interested himself in reforms, even desperate reforms; that he brought to politics itself a sense of duty and of responsibility that was not without idealism.

It should be remembered, too, that it was Franklin who, when asked "What good is it?" about the first man-carrying balloon, supplied the immortal answer, "What good is a baby?"

It is in his journalism, in his literary style and in his humor that Franklin is perhaps most indubitably American. He early had the good sense to abandon The Spectator as literary model: Poor Richard's Almanack was an annual literary declaration of independence long before there was any thought of a political one. Franklin was not a stylist in the sense that Jefferson was a stylist, but if Franklin could not have written the preamble of the great Declaration, Jefferson could not have written the Speech of Polly Baker!

That Franklin was the first American humorist is universally conceded; that his humor is characteristically American is equally clear. Who but an American would have insisted, for years, on the mythical death of a rival printer, or offered to furnish Gibbon with material for a history of the rise and decline of the British Empire, or composed that disconcerting "Edict by the King of Prussia" laying claim to jurisdiction over Britain on the ground of early colonization by the Angles and Saxons, or presented the claims of Polly Baker with such dead-pan persuasiveness, or scattered those familiar aphorisms through the pages of Poor Richard?

In one thing, certainly, Franklin connects himself with a great American tradition, and that is in his passion for liberty of the mind. As a mere boy of 16 he wrote, in the Dogood Papers: "Without freedom of thought there can be no such thing as wisdom; and no such thing as public liberty without freedom of speech * * *. Whoever would overthrow the liberty of a nation must begin by subduing the freeness of speech; a thing terrible to public traitors."

And at the end of his life he could say, "I think all the heretics I have known have been virtuous men. They have the virtue of fortitude, or they would not venture to own their heresy; and they cannot afford to be deficient in any of the other virtues, as that would give advantage to their many enemies."

We have Scriptural authority that a prophet is not without honor save in his own country and in his own house; happily the observation does not apply to Dr. Franklin, and we can imagine him, in whatever Elysian fields he wanders, noting this as another count against religious orthodoxy.

When William Pierce came to sketch the members of the Constitutional Convention, he had no trouble with Franklin. "Dr. Franklin," he wrote, "is well known to be the greatest philosopher of the present age."

He was, said Jefferson, "our Patriarch, whom Philosophy and Philanthropy announced the first of men, and whose name will be like a star of the first magnitude in the firmament of heaven when the memory of those who have surrounded and obscured him will be lost in the abyss of time."

John Adams noted with astonishment Franklin's fame. "His reputation was more universal than that of Leibnitz or Newton, Frederick or Voltaire, and his character more beloved and esteemed than any or all of them * * *. There was scarcely a peasant or a citizen * * * who was not familiar with [his name] and who did not consider him as a friend to human kind. When they spoke of him they seemed to think he was to restore the Golden Age."

That, no doubt, is what he would do if we would but let him. He admonishes us, from the not-too-distant past, to reasonableness, moderation and patience. He encourages us in that pride of country which takes the form of making a just and a happy society and discourages chauvinism. He reveals to us an undismayed faith in the virtue of the people and a calm assurance in the ability of democracy to work better than other forms of government.

His faith in education is an abiding one, and his willingness to sacrifice much to education, at every level. He makes clear to us that science is the friend of man as long as man is the master of science and that its capacity for benevolence is limitless. He counsels us to conduct our relations with other peoples and countries as we conduct our personal relations, without arrogance or violence, but with good temper, good nature and modesty.

He enjoins us to preserve freedom of thought and speech and press, for he knows from experience that without these things there can be neither safety nor progress nor happiness. He counsels us against religious bigotry, but submits to us from his venerable old age that "The longer I live the more convincing proofs I see of this truth: that God governs in the affairs of men."

The Washington Legend

by John A. Krout

"I HAVE been distressed to see some members of this house disposed to idolize an image which their own hands have molten. I speak here of the superstitious veneration that is sometimes paid to General Washington." So Benjamin Rush recorded certain remarks of John Adams to the Continental Congress in 1777. If the reporting be accurate, Mr. Adams had failed, as was so often the case during his long career, to appreciate the sentiments of his fellow-countrymen. That same confidence which had inspired him to propose the appointment of the Virginia soldier-planter as Commander in Chief of the "Continental Army" was slowly transforming the Commander in Chief into the human symbol of an emerging Americanism.

The first generation of independent Americans sorely needed stirring symbols. Generally descended from men and women who had rebelled against ritualism in religion, deeply suspicious of the trappings of monarchy, and profoundly hostile to the parading of military might, they lacked the pageantry which so often and in so many countries has helped to convert the partisan into the patriot. It is not difficult to understand why their feelings toward Washington, especially after he had scorned the temptations of dictatorial power, strikingly resembled homage. On him, for a time, they lavished that personal loyalty and devotion which is one of the romantic features in the history of many a European state. Yet this historic trend toward the personification of patriotism was almost destroyed by the very structure of the American Government.

The Presidency of the United States is a political office; and George Washington, despite his strenuous efforts, could not make it otherwise. Reluctantly he was drawn, as President, into the "turbulence of faction." Many came to regard him as a petty partisan rather than a national leader. Bache's "Aurora," published by the grandson of Benjamin Franklin, described the first President as a cheat and an embezzler, and rejoiced, upon his retirement from office, that his name would cease "to give currency to political iniquity and to legalize corruption." Not until the remembrance of the political strife of these Presidential years had begun to pass from men's minds did Washington become a really vital symbol of American faith.

The process was considerably accelerated by the romantics who perpetuated the legends of the Revolutionary era and of the career of the Commander in Chief. By the time the nation was celebrating the semicentennial of its independence, they had shaped the image of Washington which was to be accepted for almost a century. Few among these early biographers were so lyrical as the Rev. Mason Locke Weems, but all could properly be described as willing idolators.

The good parson, riding the secular circuit for the Philadelphia book publisher, Matthew Carey, found ample time, as he hawked his literary wares, to gather oral tradition for his life of Washington. It was already in a second edition in 1800. Eagerly appropriating folk stories whenever they came to his notice, and embellishing them to suit his own fancy, he came to think of his travels as expeditions into history. His sharpened quill was driven by an imagination rarely restrained by considerations of accuracy; yet he took joy in preaching to the sinner and inspiring the patriot. By the time his high-flown phrases and apocryphal anecdotes had reached a fortieth edition, his book was regarded as a classic in the steadily expanding collections of the Sunday school libraries. Its author could scarcely have been more successful in inspiring a nation of hero-worshipers had he deliberately set out to do so.

The creation of the folk hero is but superficially the work of those who write. Weems' stories bore the mark of truth not because they were told with zest, but because they recorded what men and women were saying about Washington. Fantastic they might be, but they were widely believed. In the recording Weems merely elaborated details and sharpened the outlines; he was himself captured by the spirit.

Similarly, John Marshall contributed the influence of his great authority to the development of the tradition. Legalistic in tone and stilted in style, his "Life of Washington" was widely read in numerous editions after 1804; and especially in the revision and condensation for schools in 1838, which was somewhat less dull than the earlier editions. We know now, thanks to the researches of William A. Foran a decade ago, that many parts of the huge work are merely compilations from the writings of Jeremy Belknap, David Ramsay, William Gordon and others, with a judicious selection of items from the "Annual Register." Though the borrowing was extensive, the mind of Marshall is unmistakably imposed on the material, nowhere more so than in the sections which evaluate Washington's character and services. "Demi-god," the word which Parson Weems had actually used, is implicit in the Chief Justice's worshipful attitude toward the "father of his country."

Something of the same sort of veneration left its impress on Washington Irving's five-volume "Life," though it was the most spirited of the early biographies. If the author's graceful literary style was a welcome relief from Marshall's formalism, it also concealed the fact that on many points there had been little attempt to evaluate carefully the original sources. Jared Sparks' twelve volumes of "The Writings of George Washington" were available and were consulted. Yet Irving seems to have thought that even Sparks, who had followed unusual canons of editorial censorship in safeguarding his subject's reputation, had gone too far in publishing letters which might reflect upon Washington's character and actions. At any rate, the magnificent settings and colorful details were more the result of an "act of faith" than of painstaking research.

With Irving, the early romantics reached their full power. Under their hands an image had been molded, and its lines would not be seriously modified during a long generation. It was an austere image, cold and formal, dignified and imposing; but it lacked the breath of life. Thirty-five years after Irving's volumes appeared, John Bach McMaster remarked of Washington: "The outlines of his biography are known to every school boy in the land, yet his true biography is still to be prepared. General Washington is known to us, and President Washington. But George Washington is an unknown man." The romantics, for all their enthusiastic eulogies, had elevated a symbol rather than a person. It was no accident that Americans came to prefer the Gilbert Stuart likeness, known as the "Athenaeum" portrait. Highly idealized and conventional, it nevertheless portrayed more faithfully than any other the image of Washington in the minds of his fellow-countrymen.

If the biographers had gone far toward the deification of the Commander in Chief, the historians were inclined to make him the supreme leader in the Revolutionary era. So he was in the opinion of George Bancroft; and for a later generation, John Fiske vigorously confirmed that judgment. Whether one reads the acrimonious Tory views of Henry Belcher or the sympathetic Whiggism of Trevelyan or the carefully measured detachment of Lecky, the figure of the great Virginian seems to dominate the scene so far as the achievement of American independence is concerned.

At times he towers so mightily above his contemporaries that by comparison they are unjustly dwarfed, and their influence is erroneously minimized. Some thirty years ago Beveridge gave this school of thought his accolade when he wrote in his biography of Marshall: "Washington was the Government. Washington was the Revolution." In the intervening years, scores of historians and biographers have been busy trying to demonstrate how vast was the stage and how numerous the actors for the great drama which made us a nation.

So far as research and writing bear directly on Washington's character and achievement, two recent tendencies, among others, are obvious: the attempt to reinterpret his personality in terms of ordinary human experiences and the effort to place his public services in the appropriate historical setting. Neither has been completely successful. Some who undertook to humanize the heroic image, "rigid with congealed virtue," won the reader's tentative approval as he turned the pages, but in the end failed to convince him. A few of the more lusty "debunkers" merely demonstrated that they knew far more about the interests and attitudes of the twentieth century than of the eighteenth.

Their technique was to emphasize, often unduly, the commonplace habits of young Washington with the sly insinuation that there was more than met the eye. His account books, letters and other records showed that he liked to play billiards for small stakes, that he won as often as he lost at whist, loo and other card games, that he spent considerable sums for peach brandy, bowls of arrack and bottles of "Rhennish," that his Anglo-Saxon oaths when he was enraged were dreadful to hear, that he enjoyed fox hunts, shooting matches, barbecues and horse races, and that he was rather more interested in the rising American theatre than in the Anglican Church. His greatest love, apparently, was for Sally Cary Fairfax, who happened to be married to one of his best friends. For all this substantial supporting evidence exists; but the latter-day "romantics" so exaggerated phrases and incidents, notably those relating to Sally Fairfax, as to create distortions more serious than the fantasies of Parson Weems.

In the main, their failure may be attributed to a false premise: namely, that it is possible to interpret an eighteenth-century gentleman, who early learned the secret of self-discipline, in terms of a genial and aggressive promoter who would have been at home in the third decade of the twentieth century. How much an under-standing of eighteenth-century America can contribute to an appreciation of Washington's personality is clearly apparent in the early chapters of his biography by Nathaniel Stephenson and Waldo Dunn.

Those who would brush aside unintelligent adulation in order to reveal the human qualities of the first President have encoun-tered difficulties with the sources. Not that there is any lack of primary evidence. From the time he was 16 until his death, George Washington kept a diary at frequent intervals; and from his nineteenth year he was a tireless writer of letters. These are now easily accessible, largely because of the editorial acumen of John C. Fitzpatrick. He edited the four volumes of the diaries in 1925, and in the years between 1931 and 1941 prepared thirty-seven volumes of letters and other writings for publication.

From such an outpouring one might expect a relatively full revelation of the mind of the author; yet that is precisely what is lacking. The diaries were usually suspended during troublous times; and they seldom tell what Washington thought. It is rela-tively easy to ascertain where he was, what he was doing, how much he was spending, what persons he had met; but there are few clues, even in the letters, to the inner workings of his mind or to the nature of his emotional life. So much of what he wrote was solely in response to the practical demands of his private and public interests. It is not strange that his biographers have fre-quently used the homely anecdote or the legendary tale in an effort to clarify situations otherwise obscure.

One question concerning the "Writings" is of paramount im-portance. It was raised in telling fashion by Bernhard Knollen-berg five years ago in his "Washington and the Revolution: A Reappraisal." Can the statements of the Commander in Chief concerning the men and events of the Revolution be accepted as "unimpeachable truth"? Concentrating on the relation of Wash-ington to the Continental Congress and to General Gates and General Conway, Mr. Knollenberg has come to the conclusion that the leader of the Continental forces, despite his qualities of greatness, was determined to prove himself always in the right, a trait which "led him to shift responsibility for his errors to others and to be unduly suspicious of the motives of those who ventured to criticize or differ with him."

So serious a charge, reasonably presented and carefully documented with supporting evidence, cannot be lightly dismissed. It calls for further appraisal which may go far toward a better understanding of Washington's military capabilities and his role in the winning of independence.

No one can state with precision how the last quarter-century of research and writing concerning Washington has affected popular attitudes. Certainly he appears less frequently as the unapproachable demi-god and more often as the conscientious servant of the Republic he helped to create. In the thought of many his career has become an inspiring example rather than an unattainable ideal. Whatever the differences of viewpoint among biographers and historians, all seem to agree that his courage in commonplace things and in the crisis, his gift for inspiring confidence in his fellows, his determination that his military arm should always be subordinate to the civil, his conviction that the permanence of the Union required a central Government of adequate power—that all these have become more significant with the passing years.

"A simple gentleman of Virginia," says Professor Morison, "with no extraordinary talents had so disciplined himself that he could lead a divided people into ordered liberty and enduring union." How much nobler a heritage for Americans of this generation than the mythical symbol once fashioned by romantic biographers!

Was Washington the Greatest American?

by Dumas Malone

PRESIDENT EISENHOWER has described George Washington as "the greatest human the English-speaking race has produced." This sweeping claim invites consideration in the light of history.

How does Washington really rank among the leaders of the British peoples? No one will question his title as our first great national hero, but was he first in point of time only? In the city that bears his name his monument towers above all others, but does this physical fact correspond to historical judgment? No one can answer such questions with scientific precision, but historians can employ their customary criteria and come up with interesting comparisons if not with firm conclusions.

It is desirable to narrow the field somewhat. Besides covering a lot of ground and time, President Eisenhower seems to include all categories. Perhaps we may compare Washington with Queen Elizabeth I, but we cannot well compare either of them with William Shakespeare or Sir Isaac Newton. Achievements in statecraft, literature and science are incommensurable.

Perhaps the President was thinking of greatness largely in terms of character, but he could hardly rule out achievements altogether. Probably he was thinking primarily of statesmen, including those who were also military commanders. In the English-speaking world he would have to allow for the Duke of Marlborough, William Pitt and Sir Winston Churchill, among others.

One striking parallel at least can be drawn between the most eminent living statesman of great Britain and the first great hero of our own Republic: each served as the symbol of the hopes and determination of his people in their darkest hour. With Churchill, preeminently, this was during the Battle of Britain when he summoned his countrymen to heroism by offering them blood, sweat and tears. With Washington, supremely, it was during the American Revolution when he rallied his ragged Continentals and kept the flickering flame of independence alive by sheer force of personality. The Prime Minister inspired his people with an eloquence beyond the power of Washington, while the General had to rely on his unconquerable will, endless patience and sacrificial example, but they both embodied the noblest traditions of their race.

In the present discussion we shall stay on this side of the Atlantic, disregarding Sir Winston as well as William Shakespeare, and measuring Washington against his own countrymen of the historic past. We are justified in limiting the field to statesmen (including those who have been soldiers) because in our history, certainly until relatively recent times, chief eminence has been gained in public life.

In Washington's own day nobody thought of comparing any American to him except possibly Benjamin Franklin. As Jefferson believed, the world had drawn a broad line between these two and the residue of mankind, and, as John Adams not unnaturally complained, the common opinion was that they constituted the American Revolution in their own persons. But probably the only place where Franklin's fame matched Washington's was France, and very early in the first Presidency the aged and ever-witty doctor went to his reward.

That Franklin belongs in the topmost bracket of eminent

Americans is unquestionable, but to many he seems more a colonial than a national figure. Furthermore, there was a certain earthiness about him; he was a fount of worldly wisdom; though one of the most amiable and delightful of men, he was not the sort of person to become the symbol of a people's aspiration. Even if the significance of these personal qualities should be disputed, this man of science and letters operated in a different sphere from Washington, and the first President can be more readily compared with his own successors.

If we accept the results of a poll of historians conducted several years ago by Prof. Arthur M. Schlesinger Sr. of Harvard, six Presidents of the United States are bracketed together as "great Presidents." In chronological order the big six are: Washington, Jefferson, Andrew Jackson, Lincoln, Wilson and Franklin Roosevelt. It may be added that the big five of the Dictionary of American Biography—as shown by the length of the articles —were the same except that Franklin appeared instead of Jackson, and that Franklin Roosevelt was living at the time this work was compiled and was therefore ineligible.

Without prejudice to the claims of Wilson and the second Roosevelt, I will exclude them from the present discussion—partly because they are still too close to our time for objective judgment, partly because they are too far from Washington's time to be easily compared with him. I will speak briefly of Jackson, and rather more fully of Jefferson and Lincoln.

One reason for bringing in Andrew Jackson is that there are certain parallels between him and Washington which do not exist in the other cases. He also was a military hero—the most famous Indian fighter of his generation and the supreme hero of the War of 1812. When he got into politics "Old Hickory" was virtually unbeatable; after his re-election in 1832 someone said that he could be President for life.

Perhaps in describing him as the "People's Friend" some historians have not said quite enough about his being the "Nation's Hero," but he differed from Washington in being less than a universal Hero. From the battles of Horseshoe Bend and New

Orleans onward he enjoyed enormous popularity, but as President he made many enemies. He was depicted by cartoonists as a tyrant. Though the merits of the controversies in which he engaged are still disputed, he has emerged as a man of enduring fame, and this is all the more remarkable since he faced no such fully recognized national crisis as Lincoln, Wilson and Franklin Roosevelt did.

But his fame differs from that of Washington in kind as well as in degree. It was that of a dauntless fighter, not that of a presiding genius. His times did not permit him to remain above the storms of political controversy as Washington uniquely did during most of his Presidency, seeking to preserve national unity when this was of supreme importance. Neither did Jackson's temperament permit it, and, while many saw nobility in the gaunt old man, no one could justly claim that in character he ever rose to the same height of grandeur as Washington.

One index of the popular fame of Andrew Jackson is the number of places named for him throughout the United States; in this respect, though behind Washington, he is ahead of Jefferson. The "rocking-horse" statue of him in Lafayette Square before the White House is inadequate as a national memorial, even though it perpetuates in stone his most famous words: "Our Federal Union: It Must Be Preserved." But there is no present likelihood that temples comparable to those to Lincoln and Jefferson will be erected in his honor in the national capital. These memorials complete the triangle which has its apex in the Washington Monument, and these men may be said to comprise our historic trinity of immortals.

Jefferson was the last to be admitted to it, and in the minds of some his title may be less than clear. He never presumed to put himself in Washington's class and, despite his wide popularity during his first term as President, he was never regarded as a national Hero. It is doubtful if he got much credit for his authorship of the Declaration of Independence until long after he penned it, and during his years as a national leader he became embroiled in much controversy, though he disliked it almost as much as Washington did. Even at the height of his acclaim, soon after the Louisiana Purchase and his triumphant re-election, he had many bitter enemies.

There were many murmurings of discontent against Washington during the Revolution, but after the Conway Cabal the General was unrivaled and from the final victory onward he was universally acclaimed. His second election to the Presidency as well as his first was unanimous. Leaders who sharply differed on public issues were fully agreed on him, and his countrymen as a whole looked upon him as an uncrowned king. Some very harsh things were said about him toward the end of his Presidency, but these largely boiled down to the charge that he was a "front" for Hamilton and generally they turned out to be boomerangs.

The overwhelming majority of his people retained the conviction that he himself was above criticism. He believed that his fame had withered, but it withered little and was soon restored. After his death he again became a universal hero and he has been virtually that ever since.

Jefferson enjoyed notable contemporary esteem, along with bitter hostility, and he was the recognized symbol of American democratic ideals when he died. The course of his fame thereafter has not been charted and perhaps cannot be, but he seems to have been partially eclipsed after the Civil War. One may read too much significance into the building of the memorial to him in the national capital, but the 200th anniversary of his birth in 1943, when that memorial was dedicated, may be regarded as the date of his canonization. There can be no possible doubt of the great growth of his fame in our time.

This can be attributed, I think, to two main causes. For one thing, his extraordinarily diverse interests have been made widely known by scholars and writers and by visitors to Monticello. Thus Americans have re-discovered an endlessly fascinating person who seems to have something to offer everybody. The same cannot be said of George Washington, whose genius was that of balance rather than diversity and whose lineaments seem frozen.

A second and more important reason for the present-day appeal of the author of the Declaration of Independence is that he has been seized upon as our best historic symbol of the universal and timeless struggle for human freedom against tyranny in any of its many forms. Washington symbolized national independence; Jefferson symbolizes individual independence as well, and in our age, when totalitarianism threatens, he is our most inspiring historic voice. To a greater extent than Washington, to a greater extent perhaps than any other statesman of our past, he really lives on—not so much because of his deeds or even his personality as because of his ideas and sense of values.

Jefferson's personal character withstands close examination, but as a human being he commands respect and admiration rather than the awe that Washington inspires or the affection that Lincoln evokes. One readily applies to him such adjectives as "fascinating," "stimulating" and "inspiring," and certainly he was not ignoble; but the term "noble" is best reserved for Washington, just as the word "beloved" had best be saved for Lincoln. All three of them were good men in the fullest and truest sense and each in his own way was a very great man. These differences make any precise rating of them little more than an expression of personal preference.

In Professor Schlesinger's poll the historians were asked to rate these men as Presidents. In that poll Lincoln got more votes as a "great President" than Jefferson, more even than Washington. Indeed, everybody voted for him. It must be noted, however, that Lincoln owes his fame to his Presidency to a much greater degree than either of the others. Washington was heralded as the Father of his Country because of his services in the Revolution, and Jefferson's own list of his most memorable achievements mentioned none from his Presidency.

Just how a panel of historians would vote on the relative greatness of these three men, considering their entire careers and their personalities, I do not know, but I think it a safe guess that Lincoln would get the largest vote if the question were presented to the entire electorate. There can be little doubt that he is now first in the hearts of his countrymen. To them he is still more vivid as a person than Jefferson, and far more vivid than Washington. To most people a comparison between Washington and Lincoln would really be between a colossal statue and a living legend.

It is a human tendency to make symbols out of prominent public men and to build legends around them. The Washington legend was fully formed more than a decade before his death, and since his death it has been fixed.

By contrast, the Lincoln legend was largely posthumous and it waxed with the passing years. There is nothing like it in our history, for Lincoln has come to be regarded not merely as the symbol of the Union and the emancipation of the enslaved but as the personal embodiment of our democracy and the mirror of our humanity. He has been deemed Christlike in his compassion, and his martyr's death has symbolized vicarious atonement. To criticize him in public would be the height of indiscretion, if not an act of impiety.

Historians have found in Lincoln, especially in his pre-Presidential years, more astute politics and less moral elevation than idolators have liked; but, while unwilling to view him as either a saint or a god, they greatly admire and like him. If he had not been a shrewd politician he never could have been elected President, or maintained himself in office, or saved the Union. And in his finest moments, in his Gettysburg Address and second inaugural, he reached heights that his most illustrious predecessors did not attain. Part of the perennial appeal of Lincoln lies in his angularity, in the sharp contrasts of his career and personality.

Washington, besides being well-proportioned in figure, had attained notable symmetry of character by the time he became a legend. The struggle that lay behind his self-mastery was not visible. The traits of his that were most remarked upon were prudence, fine judgment and inflexible justice.

He was a dashing horseman but, at the height of his career, most that he did was undramatic. (His feat in crossing the Delaware may be regarded as an impressive exception.) As his biographer, Douglas Freeman, says, his task as general required "patience and determination, inexhaustible and inextinguishable." Over his calendar was continuously spread the "monochrome of administrative labor." He gained a degree of public confidence that has never been approached by any other American leader—partly because he eventually succeeded but chiefly because he deserved it.

There is no better characterization of Washington than one that Jefferson made when he himself was past 70 and the first President had been dead nearly a decade and a half. It was based on an acquaintance of thirty years and the author said he would vouch for it at God's judgment seat. Here are some of the comments:

"His mind was great and powerful, without being of the very first order; * * * and as far as he saw, no judgment was ever sounder. It was slow in operation, being little aided by invention or imagination, but sure of conclusion.

"He was incapable of fear, meeting personal dangers with the calmest unconcern.

"His integrity was most pure, his justice the most inflexible I have ever known.

"His temper was naturally high toned; but reflection and resolution had obtained a firm and habitual ascendancy over it. If ever, however, it broke its bonds, he was most tremendous in his wrath.

"His person, you know, was fine, his stature exactly what one would wish, his deportment easy, erect and noble; the best horseman of his age, and the most graceful figure that could be seen on horseback.

"On the whole, his character was, in its mass, perfect, in nothing bad, in few points indifferent, and it may truly be said, that never did nature and fortune combine more perfectly to make a man great, and to place him in the same constellation with whatever worthies have merited from man an everlasting remembrance. For his was the singular destiny and merit, of leading the armies of his country successfully through an arduous war, for the establishment of its independence; of conducting its councils through the birth of a government, new in its forms and principles, until it had settled down into a quiet and orderly train, and of scrupulously obeying the laws through the whole of his career, civil and military, of which the history of the world furnishes no other example."

It is no wonder that President Eisenhower falls into the superlative mood when speaking of the great gentleman who has remained until this day the model of the republican commander and magistrate. For all time Washington set the American standard of the subordination of the military to the civil authority. He employed his unexampled personal prestige, not for his own aggrandizement, but to establish and maintain the Union. He established the Executive branch as coordinate with the Legislative, dignifying the Presidential office and guarding its prerogatives while scrupulously respecting those of Congress.

And, great as his deeds were, he himself was greater. He erred like other men, but, as Jefferson said, he erred with integrity. Personally, I feel more at home with Jefferson and Lincoln than with this formidable being, but I am not yet willing to place either one of them ahead of Washington. On balance, he still seems the greatest of historic Americans, and he would be hard to match in any country during the two centuries since he became a man.

A Reappraisal
of Alexander Hamilton

by Dorothie Bobbe

THE YOUNGEST of the Founding Fathers will be given bicentennial honors this Friday and, by Government decree, for the rest of the year. No one did more for all Americans than Alexander Hamilton, yet long-standing misconceptions about his character —his ambition, his supposed aristocratic leanings and opportunism —frequently prevent our appreciation of his extraordinary achievements.

Hamilton served as a Continental soldier throughout the American Revolution, rising to the rank of lieutenant colonel at not much more than 20, becoming General Washington's chief aide and, as one of his colleagues called him, "the pen of our army."

After the peace he entered law and politics, and represented New York at the Philadelphia Constitutional Convention of 1787—most of the time unofficially, for New York withdrew his credentials as soon as it learned that the Convention planned Federal union. Hamilton, however, had helped bring the Convention about by means of an able resolution calling for a gathering with powers wide enough to meet the states' post-war

From the *New York Times Magazine,* January 6, 1957, copyright © 1957 by The New York Times Company.

problems, and he served on the committee that drafted the Constitution itself. But his outstanding service in connection with the document was performed outside Independence Hall. It took the form of the essays, still a guiding light here and abroad, known as "The Federalist."

They were a series of newspaper pieces, addressed specifically to "the People of the State of New York," but circulating through the press of all the states. Conceived by Hamilton, who wrote the major part, although John Jay and James Madison contributed, these so-called "letters" explained the Constitution in terms of simple candor and great persuasion. In all thirteen states, constitutional conventions were meeting, most of them bitterly opposed to ratification. Independence had taken on a new meaning since the war. Centralized government, the opposition argument ran, sounded too much like old times under British rule.

In "The Federalist" Hamilton undertook to show the man in the street how together the states could overcome their ills. His "letters" did more, through their ordinary readers, to induce those assembled at the conventions to ratify the Constitution than all the speeches combined.

But the speeches counted, too. Up against an overwhelmingly antagonistic majority at the New York convention, Hamilton personally led a furious fight for ratification. Without New York, Federal union could not have been put into effect, although, technically, sufficient states had ratified before her. Even delay on New York's part would have foundered the whole. Hamilton alone was responsible for the timely accession of this most important state.

Union brought Hamilton greater responsibilities. President Washington remembered that he had shown impressive insight in the way of concrete proposals for dealing with the ruinous state of the general finances while still in the Army, and put him at the head of a newly authorized Department of the Treasury. The national finances were in an even worse state now, and threatened to nullify the victory. Credit was dead. Hard money had disappeared. At the first session of the First Congress of the United

States, Hamilton was asked to prepare an over-all financial plan. At the second session he submitted it. It called for funding the debts of Congress and for taking over the equally chaotic debts of the states. It provided for payment of both, in full, by means of Federal taxation, a Federal tariff on certain imports, the sale of public lands and the floating of Government bonds. Vehement opposition arose at once. In full, indeed! The I. O. U.'s, for one thing, were wildly depreciated through some men's speculation in other men's despair. Were gamblers to profit?

Hamilton insisted that payment at par was the only path to full faith and credit everywhere. With strong aid in both houses he fought his funding plan through, against Congressional opposition led by Representative Madison. Madison proposed payment in part to the present, in part to the original, holders of the notes. Hamilton pointed out that part payment to anyone must mean part confidence from everyone.

With his other proposition—that the Government take over the debts of the states—Hamilton had the help of Thomas Jefferson, just returned from France to be Secretary of State. Facing defeat, Hamilton had buttonholed Jefferson in the street one day and convinced him that this final assurance to prospective creditors was requisite. Jefferson invited him to dinner, together with some opposition Southerners who sought a favor from Hamilton. They wanted a capital nearer home than New York, where the Government was then located; specifically, a capital on the Potomac. Hamilton agreed to help, and did so despite the outrage of New York. In return, enough Southern votes were changed to pass Hamilton's plan for settling state debts.

There was a surge of confidence, at home and abroad. New Government bonds circulated like cash. Domestic specie hoards came out from under the bed. New foreign loans were forthcoming. Americans were induced to pay Federal taxes; and the nation found its feet.

Hamilton went on to propose organizing a Federal bank, and promptly came into violent collision with Jefferson, who believed in a strict and literal interpretation of the Constitution; otherwise,

Jefferson maintained, the states would live in constant peril from the inroads of Congress. Hamilton's scheme, he said, was unconstitutional, because a bank was not specifically authorized by the document. The Bank Bill had actually passed both houses by then, and was up for President Washington's signature. Alarmed by the word "unconstitutional" and by the passion in Jefferson's pronouncements, the President made both him and Hamilton write their opinions down.

Hamilton wrote that the power of the Government to implement all its necessary measures with the requisite means, except for specific restrictions, was implied; and under this doctrine President Washington signed the bill. Ever since, Hamilton's theory has been the model for constitutional construction. Otherwise, modern Federal legislation would have been impossible.

In winning his victories, Hamilton made enemies. Their slanders still stick to his memory. Their attack came in the course of the second Presidential campaign, when Hamilton was at the height of his power, George Washington's right-hand man, with his finger in every pie. The Federalist party was his. The Treasury Department, embracing the whole financial structure of the United States, was his. Every other governmental department felt his touch.

Jefferson distrusted Hamilton's power. Madison, once Hamilton's *alter ego,* detested it. So did Aaron Burr, a rising light in New York politics and avowedly Hamilton's friend. With the outbreak of the French Revolution, followers of Jefferson, the friend of France, began charging that Hamilton loved England; that, as Jefferson revered the common man, so Hamilton detested him.

The calumny had its roots in the Constitutional Convention, where Hamilton tentatively had called for a "Governor" of the United States to serve for life or during good behavior, a Senate on the same terms, and a lower house elected directly by the people each three years. What he had said was, "Give all power to the many, and they will oppress the few. Give all power to the few, and they will oppress the many." But he had made the mistake of praising the British Constitution for balancing one against the other. For this and nothing more, many of his opponents, including Jefferson, who had not even been present at the Convention, called Hamilton a "monarchy man" who secretly plotted kings for the United States.

It is still believed that he longed for autocrats, yet he wrote, "If I were disposed to promote monarchy, I would mount the hobbyhorse of popularity; I would cry out 'usurpation,' 'danger to liberty,' etc., etc., and 'ride the whirlwind and direct the storm.' " He warned repeatedly that the difference between demagogues and dictators is small, and that Americans should always fear the former for that reason. His enemies called him "England-lover," but his early kind words were counterbalanced when he said the King's ministers were "knaves or fools" for offering a treaty strongly favoring themselves in 1794. His political competitors said he detested the masses, yet his Federalist papers are a particular heritage of the common man, to whom they were respectfully addressed.

It was charged against him that he grew wealthy at the nation's expense. The fact is that to accept a Cabinet post at $3,000 a year he gave up a law practice bringing him three times that sum. Thereafter he would always be financially embarrassed, and though he resumed a lucrative practice toward the end of his life, he died in debt. His enemies said he cultivated the rich for personal gain. Actually, to tie the few who still had cash to the fortunes of the nation, he courted them—on behalf of the nation. He gained nothing. He would not even accept money from his wealthy father-in-law, Gen. Philip Schuyler.

He was charged with advocating factories because he despised the common man. He did indeed urge the nation to embrace industry. He knew that true independence would never be achieved until the country had a balanced economy. But most Americans were farmers and wanted to stay that way. Jefferson himself believed that only thus could they remain their own masters. Let England do the manufacturing, as before. But one day Jefferson would come to see it Hamilton's way.

Hamilton's assistance to the merchants was called part of his scheme to exploit the masses. But Hamilton made both merchants and masses secure by insisting on Federal regulation and support of purely American commerce.

He was accused of advocating severe repression of the rank and file; and this, too, is still given credence. True, he supported President John Adams' hated Alien and Sedition Acts, making a crime of criticism of the Executive, among other things, but he opposed enforcing them. Fearing and detesting mobs, he yet said, "Let us not resort to tyranny, for tyranny is worse than violence."

He was charged with being blinded by hatred of Jefferson; yet when Jefferson and Burr, of Jefferson's own Democratic party, were tied for the Presidency in 1801 Hamilton did not seize his chance. The vote was thrown into the House of Representatives, where disappointed members of the defeated Federalist party began listening to the siren song of Burr, who made them secret promises in an effort to win first place over his own leader. He was willing to bargain with Hamilton himself. But Hamilton wrote to wavering Federalist Congressmen recommending Jefferson, whose patriotism he respected. He had long mistrusted Burr, who once had told him, "All things are moral to great souls." Hamilton's letters tipped the balance in Jefferson's favor. Burr became Vice President.

Hamilton's alleged opposition to civil liberties is an equally unjust charge. In 1803 he conducted the appeal in the New York Court of Errors of a country editor named Crosswell who had been convicted under the apparently indestructible ancient British legal axiom, "The greater the truth the greater the libel." Hamilton argued, "The liberty of the press consists in the right to publish with impunity truth with good motives, for justifiable ends. That is essential to free government. To disallow it is fatal. . . . Let me remind you that the doctrine of excluding the truth as immaterial originated in a tyrannical and polluted force: the Court of Star Chamber. . . ."

Crosswell lost his appeal, but political differences also were lost in praise of Hamilton's stand. Two years later the very words he had used in court on the freedom of the press became part of the Constitution of the State of New York. Nearly all the other states have since followed suit.

Tragically, Hamilton was not finished with politics. In 1804 he used his personal influence to prevent Burr from becoming Governor of New York because he feared that Burr's ambition was to lead a Northern Confederacy out of the Union. Within four months Burr challenged him for one of many adverse remarks. Hamilton would not retract, although opposed to dueling and actually holding his fire. Thus Hamilton fell.

Had he lived on he might have obliterated some of the legends. He loved philosophy, the arts and sciences, and could have found common ground with former foes. Washington, Adams and Jefferson all managed to do so in old age. Hamilton was still less than 50 when he died, and still contending. So, to this day, the slanders invented by politicians in the heat of campaigns endure; but they cannot dim the luster of the great service Hamilton performed.

Jefferson—Man for Our Times

by Allan Nevins

A TALL, LANK, sandy-haired man of 35 sits in Philadelphia, in a three-story house newly built in a field a quarter of a mile from what is now Independence Square. He has rented for thirty-five shillings a week a furnished parlor and bedroom. Here he has set up a desk made from his own design by a cabinetmaker of the town; and with a quill pen he is busily writing a paper headed "A Declaration." He has been chosen for this task because he has maintained in Congress, as John Adams observed, "a reputation for literature, science, and a happy talent for composition." As he writes, he consults no book or pamphlet; nothing but a memory well stored with his favorite authors—Coke, Sydney, Harrington and John Locke. What he writes contains in one sense little that is new—any more than did Magna Charta. But when on Monday, July 8, 1776, it is publicly read from Rittenhouse's astronomical platform by a naval captain named John Hopkins, the crowd is enraptured. And as the public prints scatter it broadcast it is hailed with enthusiasm as a political masterpiece.

This is the historical scene by which Jefferson has chiefly cap-

From the *New York Times Magazine,* February 21, 1943, copyright © 1943 by The New York Times Company.

tured the world's imagination. But it is rightly so only if the significance of the Declaration is rightly understood. It was not a mere political manifesto converting the colonies into a new nation. Lincoln, when asked in 1859 to attend a Jefferson celebration in Boston, placed his finger on the truer and weightier meaning of the document. Jefferson, he wrote, "had the coolness, forecast and capacity to introduce into a merely revolutionary document an abstract truth applicable to all men and all times, and so to embalm it there that today and in all coming days it shall be a rebuke and a stumbling block to the very harbingers of reappearing tyranny." Nor did this abstract political truth stand alone. Jefferson was able later to ask that he be remembered also as author of the Virginia statute for religious freedom—a stroke against ecclesiastical tyranny—and as father of the University of Virginia—a blow against intellectual bondage.

Jefferson's continuing influence is a part of our national wealth. In spite of changes that seem hostile to its spirit, it has not diminished but grown. He hoped and believed that the nation would remain predominantly rural; but it has become predominantly urban and industrial. He thought that the government should remain decentralized and should interfere as little as possible with individual freedom; but it has become highly centralized, and touches every activity and interest of the people. He held that the United States should keep itself detached from European affairs; but it has become inextricably entangled with them. Yet for all his failures of foresight, his influence is still of unexampled potency. It probably outweighs that of all our other Presidents from Adams to McKinley thrown together. Why?

Because Jefferson was our most eloquent apostle of democracy, and even while our government has become centralized and bureaucratic, our faith in democracy burns more fiercely than ever. Because he always defended and extolled a mild type of revolutionary change, insisting that the cake of custom must constantly be rebroken to permit new and better institutions to struggle up; and this is a revolutionary era. Because, of all our statesmen, he was not only the most interested in political, social and moral theory but the most idealistic in his theorizing; and idealism is eternally refreshing. Because his omnivorous curiosity and versatile tastes led him to explore science, music, art, history, mechanics, agriculture and architecture, so that his writings furnish points of stimulating contact with the most varied groups. Because, with all his many faults, he was not only honest, affectionate, pure-hearted and helpful in daily life, but was singularly constant in his principal convictions, never yielding to pressure; and the world always admires moral courage.

In a sentence, his influence lives because he was one of the great liberators of the human spirit. This aristocrat who was reared on the Virginia frontier and who became one of the chief cosmopolites of his era believed in the perfectibility of mankind and its right to seek perfection. Divest struggling humanity of the manacles of superstitution and tyranny, give it a sound education and a free government, and it will attain its proper heritage of wisdom, benevolence and happiness—so he taught. Republicanism seemed to him the best of all governments, for it was the most hostile to oppression and it did most to call into play the free energies of its people. But to him political institutions mattered less than the people's will and its right to control them. "We of the United States are constitutionally and conscientiously democrats," he wrote. With liberty, peace, education, free discussion and a recognition that "institutions must go hand in hand with the progress of the human mind," mankind might rise to any heights.

There are times when nations need rest, stability and a consolidation of their gains. Such times the spirit of Jefferson, except in so far as he was a lover of peace, science and the arts, hardly fits. In certain eras the conservative ought to be dominant, for he, too, has a constructive part to play. In Jefferson's own time the more conservative groups proved that fact in the Constitutional Convention, toward whose handiwork he was distinctly cool. They proved it again in Washington's Administration, when the President and his brilliant lieutenant Hamilton did a work which Jefferson egregiously failed to appreciate. If we take the will of the masses as a touchstone, the conservative more frequently represents the majority than does the radical; for the masses are too numerous and too inert to move forward rapidly. Jefferson himself more than once got out of touch with the sentiment of the nation he was leading, while as the Sage of Monticello he survived into an era that was anything but revolutionary.

But there are other times (and this is one of them) when mankind strikes its tents and takes up its questing march; and when such periods come the spirit of Jefferson is again in the van and his maxims pass as watchwords down the columns. Every believer in reform and progress turns again to his immortal statement of personal faith: "I have sworn upon the altar of God eternal hostility against every form of tyranny over the mind of man." It is astonishing to observe how well his doctrine refits the successive crusades of the common man. When the Free Soilers in the Eighteen Fifties took up the battle against chattel slavery in earnest they turned to the great Virginian for inspiration.

Largely in honor of the man who by his clause in the Ordinance of 1787 had been first to limit slavery, they readopted the name of Jefferson's Republican party. "The principles of Jefferson," said Lincoln, "are the definitions and axioms of free society." When the agrarian revolt gave birth to populism, and populism in turn helped to produce progressivism, once more Jefferson was the great exemplar of the two movements. And today, when the bloodiest of chapters is being written in man's unending struggle, his doctrines speak to the whole democratic world with special eloquence.

Nothing could be farther from the truth than the idea that Jefferson was a magnificent theorist and little more; that his true appeal was to the emotions, not the intellect; that he was a dreamer, not a realist. His fertile, restless mind was eminently practical. It gave us the decimal units of our coinage, the Lewis and Clark expedition, a working university plan of high merit, a succession of useful laws. He loved to introduce new seeds, new agricultural methods, new sciences. "The greatest service which can be rendered to any country is to add a useful plant to its culture; especially a bread grain; next in value to bread is oil."

In his "Notes on Virginia" he furnished a perfect cyclopedia of practical information upon his native Commonwealth; he made Monticello both an exquisite piece of architecture and a museum of mechanical contrivances; he devised an improved moldboard for a plow; his books became the nucleus of the modern Congressional Library. His foresight often far excelled that of his own generation. Saying of slavery that he trembled "to remember that God is just," he did his utmost to place Virginia and upper South on the road to gradual emancipation; and had he succeeded he might have averted the Civil War. If his vision was sometimes fantastic, it was more often eminently clear and sane—and it was always vision.

Nor are his errors to be scrutinized without due consideration of the forces that helped produce them. His dislike of "the mobs of great cities" has proved unwarranted, but great cities (and especially the one he knew best, Paris) were not then what they are today. His statement that government should do nothing for men but restrain them "from injuring one another" was most inadequate; but it was not then clear how variously government could help men. In the great fundamentals, moreover, he was sound. He was, above all, sound in trusting the plain people at a time when most educated observers believed that the masses were necessarily ignorant, brutish and excitable, that egalitarianism tended to produce looseness in morals and chaos in politics and that democracy was an uneasy experiment. He was sound in holding that once a people is educated by good schools, a free press and open discussion, popular government is the stablest and strongest of all forms. He was sound in declaring that "justice is the fundamental law of society."

This champion of man's inalienable rights looms up more grandly than ever as the hosts who battle for political and intellectual freedom close in upon the last strongholds of totalitarian tyranny. A few years ago, had Jefferson been among us, he might well have been depressed by the complacent inertia, the lack of faith in democracy, the unreadiness to face sacrifices in a great cause, then to be observed on every side. But today he would feel that the spiritual insurrection of which he became the principal American voice had again vindicated its power; that mankind was again claiming its rightful title deeds.

"Even should the cloud of barbarism and despotism again obscure the science and liberties of Europe," he once wrote, "this country remains to preserve and restore light and liberty to them. In short, the flames kindled on the 4th of July, 1776, have spread over too much of the globe to be extinguished by the feeble engines of despotism; on the contrary, they will consume these engines and all who work them." An ever-inspiring champion of the common man in his march to complete liberation, Jefferson holds a fame as safe as the democratic ideas that were always his primary concern. Their triumph will be his trumph.

"Jefferson Still Survives…"

by Saul K. Padover

APRIL 13, THOMAS JEFFERSON'S birthday—the 219th this year—
is a public holiday in only three states, but the chances are that
elsewhere millions of Americans and non-Americans will remember it, too. For Jefferson, who died nearly 136 years ago, looms
ever larger as a figure of special significance. His importance now
transcends national frontiers.

Americans, of course, are familiar with Jefferson as an early
statesman, author of the Declaration of Independence, and a high-
ranking Presidential Founding Father. But there is another Jefferson less well known. This is the Jefferson who, as the American
philosopher of democracy par excellence, has an increasing appeal
to non-Americans, including the world's newly emerging peoples.
The emphasis here is on Jefferson the thinker, the champion of
the universal ideal of freedom, rather than on the American
politician and statesman.

Interest in Jefferson abroad has been rising steadily ever since
World War II. In part, this has been due to a Jeffersonian
identification with (and by) Franklin D. Roosevelt, whose pop-

ularity among foreign peoples has been phenomenal. It also has been due to the advocacy of "democracy" and "freedom" as a national American credo which has served as a counterpoint to world-girding United States foreign policy.

The extent of this interest and its effects are not measurable, at least not yet. One can only note that it exists, and that it is something relatively new. Before World War II, and indeed for a time afterward, Jefferson was little known, if at all, abroad. This was true even in Western Europe, where knowledge of American history and political ideas was limited to a handful of specialists. For example, when I was a visiting professor at the Sorbonne in 1949, I found that my highly intelligent students, who were quite well versed in Pericles and Cicero, could not identify Jefferson except vaguely as *"un homme de politique américain."*

This unfamiliarity with Jefferson was soon to change. In 1956, a biography of Jefferson was published in Paris with the subtitle *"Un Militant de la Liberté."* It carried a preface by Marshal Juin, the famous war hero and member of the French Academy, who hailed Jefferson as one whose "universal spirit" was comparable to that of Pico della Mirandola and Leonardo da Vinci and who was "fervent in his democratic ideal." Under such august auspices, Jefferson may be said to have finally "arrived" in France.

At the other end of the world, in Asia, the situation was about the same. Even Nehru, a widely read man with a lifelong concern with liberty, showed little knowledge of Jefferson. In his monumental "Glimpses of World History," the erudite Indian leader casually listed Jefferson in a single sentence with other "founders of the republic" and even misquoted the Declaration of Independence as stating that "all men are born equal"—which is certainly not the way Jefferson put it. In fairness to Nehru, however, it should be pointed out that even if he had tried to inform himself about Jefferson's thought, the chances are that he would have found scant sources in the Indian libraries of the Nineteen Twenties and Thirties.

Today, information about Jefferson is easily available in India and in other parts of the world, and not only in English but also in such languages as Arabic, Burmese, Chinese, Hebrew, Japanese, Russian and Urdu. What exactly is Jefferson's appeal and what precisely does he have to offer to foreign peoples, particularly to those now going through a process of modernization?

On one level, the appeal derives from the man. Jefferson is truly a fascinating personality who arouses interest and stirs the imagination. Where else in history does one find such a combination of philosophic thought and successful action, forming, in effect, the Platonic ideal of "philosopher as king"? And a democratic king, to boot! In the past, there have been philosophical rulers, such as Frederick the Great of Prussia and Asoka of India, but rarely ever democrats freely elected. Jefferson is thus unique.

The appeal of uniqueness is reinforced by Jefferson's ample and coherent political ideology. Quite literally, there is no other man in history—Western or Eastern—who formulated the ideas of democracy with such fullness, persuasiveness and logic. It is no exaggeration to say that those interested in democracy as a political philosophy and system cannot ignore him. He raised the fundamental questions of freedom and self-government and attempted to supply persuasive answers. Even those who do not accept his postulates or are critical of his solutions must reckon with his thought.

What, then, is his thought, and how much of it is still relevant under modern conditions?

Of all the ideas and beliefs that make up the political philosophy known as "Jeffersonian democracy," perhaps three are paramount. These are the idea of equality, the idea of freedom and the idea of the people's control over government. Underlying the whole, and serving as a major premise that is occasionally explicit and always implicit, is confidence in Man.

To Jefferson, it was virtually axiomatic that the human being was essentially good, that he was plastic and therefore capable of constant improvement through education and reason and that theoretically "no definite limit could be assigned" to his continued progress—from ignorance and superstition to enlightenment and happiness. In different words, the Jeffersonian political structure is reared on faith in the possibilities of human nature. Unless this is kept in mind, Jefferson cannot be understood properly.

What did he mean by the concept of equality, which he stated as a "self-evident" truth? Jefferson did not develop a formal theory, but the idea, about which he was remarkably consistent, is scattered through his voluminous writings.

Obviously, he was not foolish enough to believe that all men are equal in size or intelligence or talents or moral development. He never said that men are equal, but only that they come into the world with "equal rights." He used the expression "natural equality of man" to point up (as Abraham Lincoln elucidated it in 1857) two propositions that are basic to the democratic philosophy.

One was that equality was a political, rather than a biological or psychological or economic, conception. It was a gift which man acquired automatically by coming into the world as a member of the human community. In Jefferson's view, equality was a "natural right" that served as an "immovable basis" for man's claims to his liberties, including that of governing himself. "The true foundation of republican government," he said, "is in the equal right of every citizen, in his person and property, and in their management."

The other aspect of equality was that of a social standard, an article of faith necessary to keep alive man's various strivings, including happiness. Jefferson held that the primary, perhaps only, legitimate object of government was "the equal rights of man, and the happiness of every individual."

Intertwined with equality was the concept of freedom. That, too, was viewed by Jefferson as a "natural right." In the Declaration of Independence he stated it as "self-evident" that liberty was one of the "inherent" and "unalienable rights" with which the Creator endowed man. In later writings, Jefferson enlarged this idea, always stressing the basic notion that the right to freedom was an integral part of man simply by virtue of his being human. "Freedom," he summed it up at one time, "is the gift of nature."

What did Jefferson mean by freedom and why was it necessary

for him to claim it as an "inherent" or "natural" right? In the concept of Jeffersonian thought, there are two main elements in the idea of freedom, each of them operating in relation to government.

There is, first of all, man's liberty to organize his own political institutions and to select periodically the individuals to run them. This is political freedom. The other freedom is personal. Foremost in the area of individual liberty, Jefferson believed, was the untrammeled right to say, think, write and believe whatever the citizen wishes—provided, of course, he does not directly injure his neighbors. "The liberty of speaking and writing," Jefferson stated publicly as President in 1808, "guards our other liberties."

It is because political and personal freedom are potentially in conflict that Jefferson, in order to make both secure, felt the need to found them on "natural right." If each liberty derives from an "inherent" right, then neither could justly undermine the other. Experience of the past, when governments were either too strong for the ruled or too weak to rule, convinced Jefferson of the desirability of establishing a delicate "natural" balance between political power and personal rights.

"There are rights," Jefferson wrote in 1789, "which it is useless to surrender to the government, and which governments have yet always been found to invade. These are the rights of thinking, and publishing our thoughts by speaking or writing; the right of free commerce; the right of personal freedom."

This brings us to the third basic element in the Jeffersonian idea; namely, the people's control over government. From the point of view of practical politics, this is an area of crucial importance.

It is paradoxical that Jefferson, who spent most of his adult years in politics, had an ingrained distrust of government as such. For the then-existing governments of Europe, virtually all of them hereditary monarchies, he had antipathy mixed with contempt.

"While in Europe [as American Minister to France]," he told a friend in 1810, "I often amused myself with contemplating the characters of the then reigning sovereigns * * *. Louis XVI was a fool * * *. The King of Spain [Charles IV] was a fool, and of Naples [Ferdinand IV] the same. They passed their lives in hunting, and dispatched two couriers a week, one thousand miles, to let each other know what game they had killed the preceding days. The King of Sardinia [Victor Amadeus III] was a fool. All these were Bourbons.

"The Queen of Portugal [the Mad Maria], a Braganza, was an idiot by nature. And so was the King of Denmark [Christian VII] * * *. The King of Prussia [Frederick William II], successor to the great Frederick, was a mere hog in body as well as in mind Gustavus [III] of Sweden, and Joseph [II] of Austria, were really crazy, and George [III] of England, you know, was in a straight waistcoat * * *. These animals had become without mind and powerless; and so will every hereditary monarch be after a few generations."

From all this, Jefferson said, "our young Republic may learn useful lessons"—that is, the avoidance of concentrated and entrenched power. His mistrust of strong and, by extension of the idea, unchecked polity was so inveterate as to amount to a political principle. "I am not," he drily told James Madison, "a friend to a very energetic government. It is always oppressive."

Government being a necessity for civilized existence, the question was how it could be prevented from following what seemed to be historically its unavoidable tendency to swallow the rights of the people and subject them to its sway. "The natural progress of things," Jefferson said, "is for liberty to yield and government to gain ground."

His answer to this ancient dilemma was to take a position at variance with much traditional political thinking. He began with the postulate that government existed for the people, and not vice versa; that it had no independent being except as an instrument of the people; and that it had no legitimate justification for existence except to serve the people.

From this it followed, in Jefferson's view, that only the people, and not their rulers or the privileged classes, could and should be relied upon as the "safe depositories" of political liberty. "No government," he wrote to John Adams, at the age of 76, "can continue good, but under the control of the people."

This key idea in the Jeffersonian political universe, as in the philosophy of democracy in general, rested on the monumental assumption that the people at large had the wisdom, the capability and the knowledge exclusively to carry the burden of political power and responsibility. The assumption was, of course, widely challenged and vigorously denied in Jefferson's day. But Jefferson never failed to assert his confidence in the character and potentialities of the common people.

Confidence in the people, however, was not enough, by itself, to serve as a safeguard against the potential dangers inherent in political power. The people might become corrupted or demoralized or indifferent. Hence, Jefferson believed that the best practice for the avoidance of tyranny and the preservation of freedom was to follow two main lines of institutional policy. One was designed to limit power, and the other to control power.

Jefferson accepted Montesquieu's conception of the division of powers. In order to put limits on power, he felt, it was best to scatter its functions among as many entities as possible— among states, counties and municipalities; and in order to keep it in check, it was to be impartially balanced among legislative, executive and judicial branches. Thus no group, agency or entity would be able legitimately to acquire sufficient power for abuse. This is, of course, the theory that is embedded in the Constitution and that underlies the American Federal system with its "checks and balances."

For the control of power, or more specifically, the governmental apparatus itself, other devices had to be brought in play. Of these, two are of special importance. They are the suffrage and elections.

Unlike many contemporaries, Jefferson believed in virtually universal or, as he called it, "general" suffrage. By this he meant "every male citizen of the comonwealth, liable to taxes or to militia duty in any county." His opinion was that the universal right to vote, the "ark of our safety," was the only "rational and peaceable instrument" of free government.

Next to the right to vote, the system of free elections was the foremost instrument for control over government. This involved, first, the election by the people of practically all high government officials, including legislators, executives and judges; and, secondly, fixed and regular periods of polling, established by law.

To make doubly sure that this mechanism would work as an effective control over power. Jefferson advocated frequent elections and short terms of office, so that the citizens would be enabled to express their "approbation or rejection" as soon as possible. "The legislative and executive branches may sometimes err," Jefferson said, "but elections and dependence will bring them to rights."

This, in substance, is the Jeffersonian philosophy—faith in the idea of equality, of freedom, and in the right to and need for popular control over government.

What, in all this, is relevant to peoples without a democratic tradition, especially those who have recently emerged in Asia and Africa?

There is no doubt that some recent events have been disheartening to believers in freedom and democracy. In Cuba last year, when Fidel Castro shouted, "Do you need elections?" the multitude yelled back, "No, no!" In Indonesia, President Sukarno rejected "liberal democracy" as being nothing but the offspring of "dying capitalism" (which "will resort to fascism") in favor of what he called *"gotong rojong"* (mutual help) democracy.

In Pakistan, Mohammed Ayub Khan extinguished the parliamentary system on the ground that "the broad masses of the people—95 per cent of Pakistan—positively do not want a return to parliamentary democracy." Similar developments have occurred in Burma, Egypt, Ghana and other new nations.

Nevertheless, Jefferson still stands. It is noteworthy that democratic and parliamentary polity has been displaced in areas where the people had no background in freedom or self-rule, and where illiteracy is generally high. But even there it is significant that the new dictatorships are usually proclaimed in the name of the people—Sukarno's "guided democracy" and Ayub Khan's "basic democracies" being cases in point.

The inner meaning of this is that the Jeffersonian assumption that men crave equality and freedom has not been denied by events. Special conditions and traditions may explain non-democratic political methods for the achievement of certain purposes, but these remain unstable wherever the notion of liberty has begun to gain ground. "The disease of liberty," Jefferson told Lafayette 142 years ago, "is catching."

The proof of this is to be found even in such societies as the Hispanic and the Islamic, with their ancient traditions of chieftainships where popular eruptions against dictatorial rule have had an almost tidal constancy. And, as for Communist dictatorships, they have not even begun to solve the question of freedom and until they do so they will be haunted by the specters of Poland and Hungary. In the long run, no people, West or East, can escape the Jefferson idea.

But it is a slow process, as Jefferson well knew. "The ground of liberty," he said, "is to be gained by inches; we must be contented to secure what we can get, from time to time, and eternally press forward for what is yet to get. It takes time to persuade men to do even what is for their own good."

Does Jefferson survive? Indeed, he does.

Von Steuben: Our First "Top Sergeant"

by H. I. Brock

THE JUDICIOUS Washington, in a moment of exasperation, once
wrote to Governeur Morris that there were three kinds of foreign
officers in his army—"mere adventurers, men of great ambition
who would sacrifice everything to promote their own personal
glory, or mere spies." He added: "I do devoutly wish that we
had not a single foreigner among us except the Marquis de Lafayette, who acts upon very different principles from those which
govern the rest."

It was just after that famous rear-guard action (from the British
angle), the Battle of Monmouth, which one foreign General,
Charles Lee, had nearly turned into utter disaster, and another,
Baron von Steuben, had ably assisted toward turning into victory.
As the Commander-in-Chief himself put it, the entire advance
from Philadelphia to White Plains had been conducted by foreign
Major Generals—Lafayette, De Kalb, Sterling, Steuben, the last
replacing Lee, who was summoned before a court-martial. Na-
thanael Greene was the only simon-pure American in the lot.
And feeling among the "native" officers ran high.

From the *New York Times Magazine,* January 27, 1929, copyright © 1929,
1957 by The New York Times Company.

This auspicious moment had been chosen by that particular foreign officer who had been aide-de-camp to Frederick the Great, who had been doing such wonders down at Valley Forge toward putting order and discipline into the Continental ragamuffins, who had behaved so efficiently at Monmouth, to try to exchange his job of Inspector General (where he was most useful), for a regular command in the line which would have stirred up a perfect hornet's nest of offended brigadiers.

The peevish letter was written on July 24, 1778. It was only on February 23, of the same year that the Prussian Baron had arrived at Valley Forge as a distinguished volunteer who did not know a word of English. It was no longer ago than May 4 that he had become officially Inspector General of the Army with a Major General's commission for the sake of the pay and the prestige. Washington had put it cannily that the Baron's "expectations as to rank extended to that" and Congress had acted accordingly. The brigadiers had behaved as long as the new Major General was not directly in their light, a mere "extra," as it were. But there are human limits. The Commander-in-Chief saw his duty and he did it.

Baron von Steuben (he says) has "the fullest title to my esteem as a brave, indefatigable, judicious and experienced officer" but his place is where he can organize the army, not disrupt it. He remained as Inspector General, and that with his wings clipped. It is an argument of how good a soldier he was that Unser Fritz's old pupil submitted with a good grace—not without rumblings of protest, of course, but in a thoroughly military manner. Presently back in Philadelphia, whither a runaway Congress has returned from York, he is working on a plan of organization for the army through the Inspector General's office—in full submission to the Commander-in-Chief. His next job is writing the first book of infantry regulations that the army of the United States ever had —the ancestor of that I. D. R. which was the plague and admiration of our recent emergency forces, the marvel of compactness for which General Merch B. Stewart is responsible.

All this is brought to mind by the fact that there is to be sold at auction this week at the American Art Galleries a remarkable collection of relics of von Steuben—letters to and from all sorts of Revolutionary worthies and even the old warrior's sword and dress uniform. These articles were kept by the family of William North, who was von Steuben's aide-de-camp and adopted son and later became Adjutant General of the army which the Prussian volunteer had done so much to transform from a mob into a dependable fighting machine. For (in spite of his outburst) Washington handsomely acknowledged von Steuben's contribution, and Alexander Hamilton is on record as admitting that it was not until at Monmouth, he observed the effect of von Steuben's drilling upon the behavior of the troops (who under encouragement of Lee's example had been just about to run away), that he realized the true value of discipline in an army.

A disciplinarian von Steuben was—an East Prussian soldier of a race of East Prussian soldiers, trained in Frederick the Great's select school of the soldier. But he was a soldier of the school of Frederick, 1740—not of the school of Potsdam, 1914. In short, he was no mere Prussian drillmaster; rather he was an accomplished international professional in the art of war and the practice of fighting. In this he was like many other eighteenth-century soldiers—able men who were not hampered by nativity in their choice of a cause, but who went where the fighting was good and served what master they liked. Von Steuben's success with the untrained American troops was based largely upon the un-Prussian gift of flexibility—the promptness with which he adapted European drill and European tactical practice to the situation which confronted him in dealing with ragged Colonials from scattered frontier communities, collected into an army without traditions, system or service of supply. It was an army, too, where the presence of many French officers forced a certain eclecticism even upon an officer with Frederick's prestige back of him.

As a matter of fact, it was the French—specifically St. Germain, Vergennes and Beaumarchais—who were responsible for bringing to America the ex-Prussian Major just three years short of 50 at the time, whom they chose to represent to innocent folk in this country as a Lieutenant General. There is no evidence that he had ever held a General's rank of any sort in any regular European service—though, he had, in fact, been Adjutant General to Frederick. He had fought in the Seven Years' War at Prague, Rossbach and Kunersdorf, where Frederick was so disastrously defeated. Here von Steuben himself was carried off a prisoner to Russia, very soon to be set free by Czar Peter III, who admired Frederick extravagantly.

Frederick William Augustus Henry von Steuben had been ten years out of Frederick's service and was fishing for a real military job when St. Germain fetched him to Paris and inveigled him to go to America. He introduced him to de Beaumarchais, Silas Deane, Benjamin Franklin and Vergennes. It was Vergennes' policy at once to restore the prestige of France—lost by Louis XV's supineness—and to hit a shrewd blow at England by appearing before the world as the champion of liberty in America. Franklin cagily refused to pay the Prussian officer's expenses across the Atlantic. But Beaumarchais came to the rescue with 1,000 louis d'or or so, and in the Fall of 1777 shipped von Steuben off to the new United States from Marseilles on the twenty-four-gun ship L'Heureux—renamed the Flamard for precaution's sake in view of English rovers and French formal neutrality—along with a cargo of munitions of war for Washington's army.

M. le Baron, like the ship, used an alias. He was called Frank, and was officially charged, in case of seizure and search, with harmless letters to the Governor of Martinique. Nevertheless, he went in a certain state. Besides Peter S. Duponceau, secretary, there were three aides. One of them, de L'Enfant, is now known to fame as the city planner of Washington. Also aboard was Beaumarchais's nephew and agent, De Francy. Ill-fortune attended the voyage, two storms and a mutiny. The Flamard had been at sea sixty days when, on Dec. 1, 1777, Baron von Steuben, dressed in British scarlet and blue—the French had told him that the Americans had stuck to the British uniform even when they rejected British rule—landed at Portsmouth, N. H., and was received with salutes of cannon. He had letters from Franklin to Washington and leading members of the Congress. John Hancock entertained him in Boston and provided him with horses for the journey to York, where the Congress was in hiding— the British being in Philadelphia and Washington at Valley Forge.

The moment was the fortunate one when the surrender of Sir John Burgoyne at Saratoga had come to relieve the deep gloom of a hard and hopeless Winter. The Baron was pleased to find that there were many people who spoke German in Pennsylvania, and to see the familiar hard mug of Old Fritz out as a sign over the doorways of inns. At Lancaster he danced gayly with the German girls. Washington rode out to meet him at Valley Forge and assigned him a guard of honor of twenty-five men, which he refused. So had the French fiction as to the European rank of the volunteer prevailed! At the moment, of an original force of 17,000, there were only some 5,000 men fit for duty, and many of the soldiers were nearly naked. Some regiments consisted of thirty men or less. Von Steuben gave a dinner to which no officer was invited who had a whole pair of breeches. It was largely attended and flaming salamanders were drunk. Von Steuben called it his dinner of "sans culottes," before the French Revolution took over the name. It was a serious camp, with no dancing or playing. When officers met socially, as, for example, at the General's quarters with Mrs. Washington, there was singing —the company "obliging" in turn.

Presently Washington had the newcomer, still a mere volunteer without rank, on the job of introducing order into the army. Von Steuben picked 120 men from the line as a guard for the Commander-in-Chief and used it as a demonstration company. He drilled it himself twice a day, taking the musket in his own hands and showing "the manner of the exercise." This performance shocked some (he says), who had the English notion that "drilling recruits was a sergeant's duty and beneath the attention of an officer."

However, except for this G. H. Q. guard, he did not undertake to meddle much with the company drill. Some officers did it the English way, some the French way, some in the German way, and each was jealous of his own way. Which is why, von Steuben explains, he reversed the usual order of military training —taught the men manoeuvres first. That seemed the practical thing to do, in view of the need of making soldiers in two months where a European army would allow three months to make mere "recruits."

As to the bayonet, he let it go for the present, because the "American never used his bayonet but to roast his beefsteak." A year later you read, upon inspection of a brigade by the Inspector General in person, that he took seven hours for the job and examined every man's piece and accoutrements, insisting on the "brightest polish" of bayonets and muskets, and never letting "the smallest spot of rust escape him."

For the present he could not even make the men understand him. For he knew no English. At his first appearance in charge of instruction the Baron was sputtering and swearing helplessly in German, when Captain Benjamin Walker of the Second New York Regiment offered his services as interpreter. Walker was greeted as "an angel from heaven" and became from that time forth the Baron's aide and interpreter.

William North tells how at this time "the Baron used to rise at 3 o'clock in the morning. He smoked a single pipe while his servant dressed his hair, drank one cup of coffee and was on horseback at sunrise." When the arrival of a French fleet off the Delaware Capes made Philadelphia untenable for the British and General Clinton withdrew through New Jersey toward New York, Washington sent von Steuben to reconnoitre ahead of his pursuing forces. While on this duty the Baron stumbled, near Princeton, upon a patrol of British light horse who seemed to have been Hessians. He escaped only by leaping a fence and running for it, and lost his hat. The next day, as the advance continued, some prisoners of this same light horse were brought in. They were produced before von Steuben, who asked why they had not fired at him. The answer was that von Knyphausen, the Hessian commander, had recognized his countryman and given orders that he be taken alive.

The manner of the composition of Steuben's Infantry Regulations adopted by Congress in February, 1779, is curious. In this work the Baron was assisted by Colonel Fleury, Captain Walker, Captain de L'Enfant and M. Duponceau. It was first written roughly in German by von Steuben, then translated into bad French, then put into good French by Duponceau and finally into good English by Walker. When it was finished, says Friedrich Kapp, in his admirable biography of Steuben, "Steuben did not understand one word of it." De L'Enfant's part in the work was making the plates showing the position of the soldier, etc.

It was just at the height of von Steuben's usefulness that the shameful defeat at Camden burst the bubble of Horatio Gates's unearned reputation and left the south at the mercy of Cornwallis's army. Steuben was dispatched to Virginia to "create a Southern army." The words are Washington's own. Why he did not achieve that particular miracle is a story in itself. When Washington executed his coup at Yorktown, it was von Steuben, commanding the first-line trenches, who received the first offer of capitulation from the British. Thence arose the dispute with Lafayette which the partisans of the two officers have kept alive to this day.

When the war was over von Steuben set up for a while in a country house in the middle of Manhattan Island in Jones's Wood, in the region of the present Fifty-seventh Street. He rented the house from one "ready-money Provost," who had built it, and it was called, for some reason, "The Louvre." Later he moved to his farm in Steubenville, where in a log house he spent his last years as a good American, grumbling at things he did not like and reading and talking with his friends as an old soldier should. He died in 1794. Something of the flavor of the so miscalled "Prussian drillmaster" appears in the following extracts from some of his letters included in the North collection: In September,

1788, with General Washington's Presidency impending, the Baron writes to North—remember that he had been Grand Marshal of a court in his time:

"Our politicians are now busy in settling the etiquette of the New Court. A Palais Royal is to be prepared. Audience and Leve days to be fixed, the ceremonies to be determined. My opinion as an old courtier has been asked. I begun by abolishing all nut-cracking after dessert. I proposed the number of bows to be received and returned and made several useful observations. As to the Queen's Leve, I say nothing. I wish it could be very late in the evening and without candle light."

Again to the same, in December of the same year:

"Everyone here is occupied to dispose of the offices according to his interest or inclination. For the great chair are candidates G. W. or God Almighty, for the second Great Adams or big Mistress Knoks. She alone disputes this place to the first of men. Chief Justice Mr. Jay, Minister of Finances, Hamilton, or Warr, the big bookbinder if his wife fails in her attempts. Of Foreign Affairs, perhaps Madison, perhaps, King Rufus—for the home department perhaps sweet Charley or some others."

Tragedy of
Arnold Revealed

by Randolph G. Adams

THE PRIVATE military records of the British Commander-in-Chief in the American Revolution have come to the United States. When it was announced some weeks ago that the papers of Sir Henry Clinton had been purchased for the W. L. Clements Library at the University of Michigan, the donor of that library and its librarian were deluged with letters from all over the United States. What news did these documents contain? What light do they throw on obscure corners and half-told stories of the Revolution?

The queries ranged from the serious to the trivial; they came from historical research scholars in the great universities and from dear old ladies who were trying to find out whether their ancestors' part in the Revolution would enable them to join some patriotic society. It will be years before all these questions are answered, because the papers are so numerous, and because many of them must be prepared with the utmost care before they can be read.

But even at this early date a few bits of news cannot help

coming out—they fairly exude from the archives which are so rich in new stories about the winning of American independence.

The treason of Benedict Arnold, with its tragic sequel, still remains one of the best-known acts of the Revolution. It is the one most frequently mentioned by orators and by writers in a search of a classical example of treachery. Yet America has had but half the story—the part that could be told from the American side. The tragedy involves the downfall of one of the bravest of American Generals; the death on the gibbet of one of the most lovable characters in the British Army and the ruin of a beautiful American woman.

The outline of the story is well known. Arnold was the dashing leader of the Americans in their victory over Burgoyne at Saratoga. His personal courage in that decisive conflict stands out in brilliant contrast beside the incompetence of the nominal American commander, General Gates, who reaped the credit for this triumph of American arms. Yet, despite his ability and accomplishments, Arnold was abominably treated by the petty politicians in the Continental Congress, who even thought of deposing Washington himself. The grievances Arnold suffered at the hands of the small men in Congress were very real. Washington was great enough to disregard his detractors; but Arnold was only human and yielded to his anger, his resentment, above all to his need for money.

Arnold Weds Peggy Shippen

When the British evacuated Philadelphia, in June of 1778, Washington appointed Arnold to command the garrison at that place. There he entered into the social whirl of a city used to gayety, and there he fell in love with Philadelphia's most charming debutante, Peggy Shippen. The marriage of this famous soldier and the darling of Philadelphia society was a great event. Visitors to Philadelphia who motor to Fairmont Park can still see the great mansion above the Schuylkill where Arnold took his bride and continued the round of dances and parties to which she had been accustomed.

Suddenly he was ordered to command the key to the American positions above New York, the fortress at West Point. Thither he went with his wife, and from that place, a few months later, he fled after a futile attempt to betray it to the British commander, Sir Henry Clinton. He was discovered in the nick of time, and fled so precipitately that he was compelled to leave behind his wife and child—also the English officer, Major André, who had to pay the penalty Arnold deserved.

Negotiated with André

The Clinton papers bring to light, at last, the inside story of Arnold's treason. Hundreds of letters and copies of letters, many in cipher, many of them masked and others in invisible ink, were sent to and from Sir Henry Clinton's headquarters in New York. The task of conducting the British end of these negotiations fell to Major John André, Adjutant General at New York. He was one of the many British officers who had also fallen under the spell of Peggy Shippen's charms during the Winter in Philadelphia.

From André's papers it became clear that Arnold began his propositions at least fifteen months before the tragedy at West Point. As soon as he had been appointed to command at Philadelphia, Arnold, smarting under the injustice he had suffered at the hands of Congress, and fearful of the French alliance which Franklin had just arranged at Paris, proposed to Sir Henry Clinton to betray the American cause. Not only did he propose to change sides, but he proposed also to bring with him the means of ultimate British victory.

A critical examination of the sources of American history seems to be continually tearing the mask from our heroes of the past. An examination of André's papers in the Clinton collection serves only to blacken yet more the character of Benedict Arnold. We have the document in which, under the alias of "John Moore," he deliberately asks for an interview "with some intelligent officer" on Clinton's staff. The British Commander lost not a moment in complying. There are now before us his letters, which do not attempt to conceal the exultation he felt at the prospect of gaining an American General and his post by treachery.

Early in the correspondence Arnold is discovered not only plotting the surrender of West Point but also sending long cipher dispatches to Clinton about the strength and movements of the American armies, and information the American headquarters had about the coming and the destination of the French fleet and French troops, which were ultimately to decide the war.

Early in the negotiations, too, Arnold shows his true colors. What he really wanted was money—cold, hard English pounds. "If I point out a plan by which Sir Henry Clinton shall possess himself of West Point, its garrison, stores, artillery, etc., I want twenty thousand pounds sterling. I think it will be a cheap purchase for an object of so much importance."

Since the British did not respond to his demands promptly enough, he states in a cipher letter that he "expects to have your promise that I shall be indemnified for any loss I may sustain in case of detection, whether the contest is finished by the sword or by treaty, and that ten thousand pounds shall be engaged me for my services." It was a case of twenty thousand if he succeeded, or half that amount if he failed.

The British commander wanted to substitute a promise for a command of "five or six thousand men" in the British Army, with twice that many thousand guineas, if Arnold was successful in his betrayal. But Arnold stuck to his original demand.

In July of 1780 the conspirators were evidently fearful of discovery. Arnold changed his name from John Moore to Edward Fox, and then again to Gustavus. André began by signing his letters Joseph Andrews, which he changed before long to John Anderson, the alias he bore when captured. Among the other revelations in the Clinton papers is the extent of the conspiracy —Arnold, Clinton and André were but three of the actors. There were at least four other British spies involved, whose correspondence illuminates the dark corners of the whole affair.

André, as an old friend of Peggy Shippen, writes directly to her "with a view of communicating information" to Arnold or to one of the British spies within the American lines. Undoubtedly, there were several of these spies actually within the American fortress all the time the negotiations were going on. Historians have usually acquitted Peggy Shippen of any complicity in her husband's treason, but the Clinton papers give many indications of another story.

A son had been born to Arnold and Peggy Shippen just before the treason. We have actual evidence of her desire to buy baby's clothing in New York, for there were no shops in West Point like those in lower Manhattan. Her list of demands for "pink ribbon" and "diaper clouting" is among the other papers, sent by one of the British spies to New York.

The spectacle of the rejected suitor, Major André, buying these articles for Benedict Arnold's baby does not usually figure in history. Yet the number of times that the wants of the Arnold baby figure in the correspondence is significant of some knowledge on Mrs. Arnold's part that her husband was engaging in a rather familiar correspondence with the British headquarters.

Ingenious Cipher Devices

The methods of cipher used are simple but ingenious. Both Arnold and André would take copies of the same book. Dispatches would then pass back and forth in which each word in the letter would be represented by three numbers. The numbers were the page number, the line number and the word number of some word in the volume agreed upon. The messages would consist of page after page of numbers.

Fortunately, the Clinton papers contain full details about the books thus employed. On one occasion they used the fifth Oxford edition of Blackstone's "Commentaries on the Laws of England."

On another occasion there would be employed the twenty-third edition of Baily's Dictionary. Sometimes they would select popular song books of the day and use them in the same fashion.

On other occasions the conspirators would employ masked letters. A sheet of paper would have cut in it an irregular hole. Another sheet exactly the same size would be placed beneath it and the message written in the part of the under sheet thus left exposed. Then the mask would be removed and the words composing the message would be surrounded with other words in such a fashion as to make a grammatical but sometimes absurdly unintelligible composition, which would look like a complete letter. Arnold and André would each have paper the same size and identical copies of the mask.

Then, too, there are messages written on tiny slips of paper, to be enclosed in specially constructed hollow bullets. In one of these Clinton had sent his famous message to Burgoyne in the previous year, and the messenger, on being captured, had swallowed it. The American officer who captured him gave the messenger an emetic.

In their communications in which Arnold was trying to betray the secrets of American troop movements, the two men sometimes adopted a special code of biblical names. Philadelphia was Jerusalem; Pittsburgh was Gomorrah. The necessity for the use of such a far-away post as Fort Duquesne shows the many ramifications of the plot. The American Generals became the twelve apostles. Washington was St. James, Sullivan was St. Matthew, Gates was St. Andrew, Judas Iscariot, instead of being Arnold himself, was the relatively innocent General Bird. The Indians were referred to as the "Pharisees" and the Delaware River was the "Red Sea." The papers contain a full list of these Biblical names and their equivalents.

Climax of Conspiracy

Work on the papers has not yet progressed far enough to determine how far the conspirators used invisible ink, but they made allusions to it, as on an occasion when the blank paper was spoiled by the damp, so that when held near the fire the message could not be read. One remembers the use of lemon juice and other such simple liquids in this connection. Edgar Allan Poe has made them famous in his "Gold Bug."

Papers covering the climax of the conspiracy are exceedingly full. Not only are there now available the letters between the chief conspirators but also the letters of the auxiliary actors like Captain Sutherland of H. M. S. Vulture, which bore André up the river to his meeting with Arnold, and numerous letters of the British and Tory intelligence officers reporting on the meeting. Then comes a blank. André is lost sight of. Suddenly comes the news that he has been caught and sent to West Point. Arnold appears in New York, a fugitive—and, at that, utterly unsuccessful in his crime.

Then comes the most pathetic part of the story. Judging by Clinton's own writings, he was in a state of consternation at what had happened to André, who was one of his warmest personal friends. The British commander kept notes from day to day during the course of André's trial, trying to justify himself and to exculpate himself from any share in the blame for André's fate. The character of these notes seems to indicate that he never intended any one to read them. When finally the news arrives that André has been executed, Clinton's handwriting in his diary becomes almost illegible. "The horrid deed is done—Washington has committed premeditated murder."

One of the greatest treasures of the collection is the last letter written by André to his Commander-in-Chief. It has been published many times, but the original pathetic document itself now rests in the library in Ann Arbor, fittingly preserved in its proper place with the other papers relating to that great tragedy. In it André frankly admits that he failed to follow his instructions and that his fate is largely due to that disobedience.

The Clinton papers contain a bulky manuscript, "History of the Campaigns in North America," written by Clinton himself. It has never been published. In it one can find Clinton's version of the affair. He records that he specifically instructed André not to change his dress (for André started out in full uniform), and not under any circumstances to carry any papers. André, unfortunately for him, did both of these things, and for that reason made himself into a spy within the meaning of military law.

Sir Henry Clinton's history has never been used by any historian. It would make at least two stout octavo volumes and is fully annotated with references to the documents in the style of the most meticulous modern scholar. What secrets it may yet reveal can only be conjectured—but it gives every American food for thought to reflect that we have had the stories of the American Revolution told and retold without ever looking at the testimony of the British Commander-in-Chief, who, next after Washington, was the principal actor. The chronicle of the Arnold-André affair in this document occupies the better part of two chapters.

The utter futility as well as folly of Arnold's treason is made abundantly clear in the nature of his dispatches to Clinton. Arnold was constantly telling Clinton that Washington and Rochambeau were going to attack New York—which they never did. Not once in all the letters is there a hint of that great concluding act of the Revolution, the possibility of Washington and Rochambeau marching swiftly south around New York and capturing Cornwallis at Yorktown.

No doubt it was these dispatches of Arnold's, and his further confirmation of them after he reached the British lines, that kept Clinton hugging New York when his presence was so badly needed in Virginia the next Summer. Arnold's treason served the American cause in an unexpected way.

In the letters the crassness of Arnold's act keeps constantly cropping out. He seemed to think that as he himself could be bought so could everyone else. He solemnly offers to go out and buy 3,000 of his American soldiers at the rate of 15 guineas per head—money to be supplied by Clinton. He argues that the British are paying more than that for the Hessians, Brunswickers and other German troops which they had brought to America. Moreover, he shrewdly points out that the killing of the Hessians costs money, as their contemptible master, the Landgrave of Hesse-Cassel, was to be given extra pay if his men died.

In cold-blooded fashion Arnold indicated to Clinton that the Germans, unused to the climate of America, were dying like flies and that the Americans would not die off that way. Further, Arnold insists that any one American soldier is worth two Germans and that under his command, given enough money, he could purchase enough of his old soldiers to put down the rebellion.

"Money, properly applied in America," he writes, "may with some have more argument than arms." He even suggests that Washington probably could be bought off with an English title.

Not the least part of the whole story is contained in the maps of the Hudson River Valley, which were prepared in connection with the treason of Arnold. They range in size from little sketches no larger than the palm of one's hand, made on horseback, to huge manuscript charts six and eight feet long. The latter are exquisite specimens of water-color work, the work of the engineer officers, Major Montressor and Alexander Mercer.

The lines at West Point; the geography of the Hudson River from Verplanck's Point and Stony Point all the way to West Point; the lines at Forts Clinton and Montgomery and all the American works and redoubts are to be seen in the utmost detail. Many of these maps are worthy of exhibition in a modern water-color exhibit.

There is a letter from Clinton to the British Secretary of War, Lord Germain, which confesses, after it was all over, the uselessness of the whole transaction. "We have not, I confess, derived from it the very great advantages I expected. The plan unfortunately miscarried, and I have paid that officer the sum of £6,315 as compensation for the losses he sustained for coming to us—which may in consequence appear large." The letter further gives grounds for suspecting that the entire business began with a suggestion from Germain himself.

It is notorious that Lord Germain was expelled from the

British Army for cowardice, and there is some evidence to show that he believed that since he could buy his way back into favor in England and buy German troops and buy seats in Parliament for the King's friends, he could also buy American Generals. There are few figures in British history more contemptible than Lord George Germain, and the Clinton papers contain hundreds of his letters to Clinton.

When the end came at Yorktown Arnold had to leave the united American territory with the British Army. If he expected gratitude in England he certainly did not get it. The average Englishman was too honorable to treat with anything but contempt the miserable victim of Lord Germain's policy of corruption. Indeed, we are begining to learn that the whole American Revolution was immensely unpopular with a substantial proportion of the British public. That proportion came into power immediately after the war and just at the time when Arnold was trying to establish himself as a loyal British subject who deserved well of the King.

Moreover, poverty followed social ostracism. We know from the papers of Judge Shippen of Philadelphia, which are in the possession of the Historical Society of Pennsylvania, that that unfortunate gentleman had to send thousands of pounds to England to keep his daughter and her husband from starvation. But the time came when even Judge Shippen grew tired of supplying Arnold with money.

Then Arnold turned again to Clinton, and the papers of that officer pick up the story once more. There are begging messages from the erstwhile American hero, complaining bitterly of the treatment he had been accorded in England—"having on many occasions received the most unmerited illiberal abuse in consequence of the decided part I had taken in the late American war, which has been imputed to mercenary rather than to the just motives which influenced my conduct"—and he begs Clinton to help him out.

Mercenary Motives

We know from the documents how rightly the British public estimated his motives. These certainly were mercenary, above anything else. In 1787 the affairs of the Arnolds had reached such a desperate state that we have the sad sight of Margaret Shippen Arnold writing a letter to Clinton in which she begs for help. The Arnold papers in the Clinton archives end with the following pathetic letter:

"May I venture to hope that the present anxiety of my mind will plead as an apology for the liberty I take in addressing you? Surrounded by a numerous little family, without the means of educating and supporting them in a style at all equal to what the former part of my life promised, and our scanty income being dependent upon our lives, by which means my children would be left to want, in a strange country in case of our deaths, you will not be surprised that every maternal feeling is awakened— and that I am deeply interested in General Arnold's present application to Mr. Pitt, the favorable event of which will no doubt in a great measure depend upon your representation of his conduct.

"From your justice I have everything to hope. May I presume to solicit your friendship? And more earnestly to entreat that you will extend it to us on the present occasion by exerting your influence with Mr. Pitt in our favor, with whom it now rests to render us easy with respect to the future fate of those most dear to us."

In many ways the one bright spot in all this sorry mess was Margaret Shippen's loyalty to Benedict Arnold.

The Men Who Signed the Declaration

by Dumas Malone

ON THE Fourth of July every year, Americans do more than celebrate the beginnings of their Republic; they honor a charter, the Declaration of Independence, which has come to be invested with the sanctity that once hedged about a king. But this sacred charter was originally a human document, prepared and adopted by living men. Thomas Jefferson is frequently mentioned at these annual celebrations, as he ought to be, and Benjamin Franklin and John Adams sometimes are; but the other "votaries of independence," as Adams termed them, are generally overlooked. The signers of the Declaration are rarely viewed as a group.

What manner of men pledged to this cause their lives, their fortunes and their sacred honor? Were they old or young, rich or poor, radical or conservative? The short answer is that there was very considerable diversity among them, but that they were nearly all men of substance and public experience, and all of them believed in freedom. They invite further description as an aggregation of human beings.

It would be an exciting experience to see them as a group, but,

From the *New York Times Magazine,* July 4, 1954, copyright © 1954 by The New York Times Company.

as a matter of fact, they were never thus assembled. If this statement seems surprising, an explanation can be found in the circumstances of the signing. The engrossed document which successive generations of Americans have seen in reproduction contains fifty-six signatures, but no one of these was affixed before Aug. 2, 1776. The Declaration was printed immediately after its adoption on July 4, and in this printed form it was attached to the Rough Journal of Congress with a wafer and circulated in the states for proclamation.

But the only names it bore were those of the President of the Congress, John Hancock, and the Secretary, Charles Thomson of Philadelphia, who attested Hancock's signature. Also, it had a different title from the one we have become accustomed to. The word "unanimous" could not yet be used, since the New York delegates, who were awaiting instructions from home, had abstained from voting. Not until July 19, when the favorable action of New York was reported, could the pronouncement be entitled the "Unanimous declaration" of the thirteen states. On that day, also, it was ordered that the document be engrossed; and on Aug. 2 it was ready for signatures. By that time some of the delegates who had voted on July 4 were no longer present; new members had arrived and were expected to sign; and further signatures were added during the next few months. There was no secrecy about membership in Congress, but the names of the Signers as such were not made public until another year had started. In January, 1777, Congress resolved that an authenticated copy of the members subscribing to it be sent to each of the states. Even so, the list was incomplete, for the name of Thomas McKean of Delaware was not on it. Presumably he did not attach it to the engrossed document until after that, and was the last of the signers.

The patriots in John Trumbull's painting, "The Declaration of Independence," were never assembled as a group on a particular day—July 4 or Aug. 2 or any other—but this fact does not detract from the value of a deservedly famous work. It is a more important consideration that the artist painted three-fourths of these historic characters from life, and we can be grateful to him for giving us most of the Signers as they looked in their own time. We can be grateful, also, for some of the colorful stories about the signing that have come down through the years. Legendary these may be, rather than historical, but often they are in character.

One of the most familiar and most engaging is associated with the incomparable Franklin. Just before the signing began, President Hancock is supposed to have observed: "We must be unanimous; there must be no pulling different ways; we must all hang together." Thereupon Franklin remarked: "Yes, we must indeed all hang together, or most assuredly we shall all hang separately." This saying appears to have got into print about half a century after the sage had died, which was much too late for him to disavow it. It is just the sort of thing he might have said, and as a witticism it certainly deserves remembrance.

Another story is told about Benjamin Harrison of Virginia, now noted as the father of one President of the United States and the great-grandfather of another, but then renowned for his bulk and his propensity for joking. To Elbridge Gerry of Massachusetts, who was small and spare, Harrison is reported to have boasted that he would have much the easier time at the hanging; his neck would be broken instantly, while Gerry would kick in the air for half an hour. This sally could not have occurred on Aug. 2, however, for Gerry was one of those who signed later.

Much better known is the story of Hancock's signing. He is supposed to have said that he wrote his name in large bold letters so that John Bull could read it without spectacles and double the reward on his head. His name, as President, had been attached to the printed Declaration that was first proclaimed, so there could be no possible secret of his participation in these revolutionary events, and actually his signature was big in his personal letters.

Hancock centered his name beneath the text. The other fifty-five signatures are grouped by states beginning with the Georgians on the left and ending with the New Englanders on the right. The order, roughly, is from south to north, reversing the customary procedure. The Pennsylvanians, nine in number, comprised the largest state group; the Virginians came next with seven; and there were five each from Massachusetts and New Jersey. Each delegation voted as a unit in Congress, regardless of its size. The number of delegates varied, and the unusually large representation of Pennsylvania does not mean that revolutionary sentiment was strongest in that state. In reality, opinion was sharply divided in the middle states and the cause of the Patriots was probably strongest in New England and Virginia.

The oldest and also the most eminent of these fifty-six men was Benjamin Franklin, recently returned from England; he was 70, while the youngest delegate, Edward Rutledge of South Carolina, was only 26. The four South Carolinians comprised the youngest of all the state groups, their average age being less than 30. Stephen Hopkins of Rhode Island was almost as old as Franklin, while the latter's colleague, Dr. Benjamin Rush of Philadelphia, in his thirty-first year, was one of the youngest men.

Jefferson, the author of the Declaration, was 33; and John Adams, recently described as the "Atlas of Independence" was in his forty-first year. Samuel Adams, who had done more, perhaps, than any other single man to foment revolt, was in his middle fifties. On the whole, these men were young or in the prime of life. They cannot be classified with precision on grounds of occupation, for theirs was not an age of specialization, and occupations constantly overlapped. Lawyers were more numerous than the members of any other profession, and such men as Richard Stockton of New Jersey, James Wilson of Pennsylvania and George Wythe of Virginia would have been an ornament to any bar.

But many of the nominal lawyers were Southern planters who really got their living from the land. By this time Jefferson had ceased to practice and some of the others seem never to have begun. All four of the South Carolinians had had legal training in England, at the Middle Temple, but they were all members of the plantation aristocracy.

By any fair standard the Signers as a group were well-educated men, though some of them had had little formal schooling. Benjamin Franklin was largely self-taught, but he had picked up the degree of LL.D. at St. Andrews and was honored throughout the Western world for his scientific attainments. Every member of the Massachusetts delegation was a graduate of Harvard, as were William Ellery of Rhode Island, William Williams of Connecticut and William Hooper of North Carolina. No other college had quite so large a contingent, but Yale, William and Mary, and Princeton were well represented. The College at Princeton had the added distinction of contributing its president, John Witherspoon, a philosopher of note and the only clergyman in Congress. This impressive man was born and educated in Scotland, and he was an exceedingly effective speaker despite his strong Scottish burr.

There were four physicians, though their attention to medicine was far from exclusive. Two of them, Josiah Bartlett and Matthew Thornton of New Hampshire, afterward became judges, while Lyman Hall of Georgia, though more engaged in practice, was at this time a rice planter and later became Governor of his state. Dr. Benjamin Rush was a man of wide interests, too, but he owes his fame chiefly to his professional activities.

The country was predominantly agricultural, and most of the Signers lived close to the soil, but there were almost as many merchants among them as planters and farmers. The names of John Hancock of Boston, Philip Livingston of New York and Robert Morris of Pennsylvania instantly come to mind. Industry was in its infancy, but a couple of the less conspicuous Pennsylvanians, George Taylor and James Smith, had iron furnaces. A few of the delegates had gained local prominence as the avowed spokesmen of back-country districts, but, as was to be expected at this stage of settlement, most of them were identified with the seaboard.

Certain men defy classification because of the range and diversity of their interests and activities. Francis Hopkinson, who now represented New Jersey though he was born and died in Philadelphia, was at the same time a lawyer, composer and versifier. In Congress he whiled away the tedium of debate by drawing caricatures, and afterward he carried on an animated correspondence with Jefferson about mechanical improvements of the harpsichord.

In 1776 the class of professional politicians in the modern sense did not exist in America, but at this stage these men were devoting themselves to public affairs. One of the most characteristic and significant aspects of their era was a widespread sense of public responsibility. In time of crisis these patriotic citizens had left their customary occupations in order to perform larger service, just as Washington had picked up his long-unused sword and ridden away from his beloved acres at Mount Vernon.

But while these men did not make a business and a living out of politics, they were too well schooled in public affairs to be called amateurs. This can be said of the youngest of them. In the Southern plantation country members of the leading families were entrusted with public duties almost as soon as they were grown. At the age of 33 Jefferson had behind him years of political experience as well as years of thought and study.

Though bold in word and action, these experienced men were responsible statesmen, not reckless adventurers, and with relatively few exceptions they were men of substance. By the standards of their time a number of them were exceedingly wealthy. President John Hancock had fallen heir to a lordly fortune and has been described as a "patriot in purple." The Pennsylvania delegates had been conspicuously slow in taking the decisive step toward independence, and John Adams, who was never a rich man, attributed their reluctance to "the timidity of two overgrown fortunes."

He was referring to Robert Morris and John Dickinson, the latter of whom left Congress and never signed the Declaration, though he did do military service. Morris signed, regardless of his fortune. Philip Livingston, who may likewise be described as a merchant prince, had disapproved of the riotous actions of the Sons of Liberty in New York, and he is generally regarded as a conservative, but he took the road to independence with the patriots when the time came.

There were plain men among the Signers, as their portraits show unmistakably. Roger Sherman of Connecticut, who had started as a cobbler, was one of them, even though he was now a well-to-do merchant in New Haven and had received an honorary degree from Yale. John Hart, oldest of the New Jersey Signers, was described by a contemporary as "a plain, honest, well-meaning Jersey farmer, with but little education, but with good sense and virtue enough to pursue the true interests of his country."

His colleague Abraham Clark may be described as a "man of the people" in a more political sense. Becoming known as the "Poor Man's Counselor," he exploited popular distrust of pretentious lawyers and gained political support chiefly because of his championship of popular rights against various forms of privilege. Samuel Adams was identified with the "popular" party of Massachusetts, and Franklin with that in Pennsylvania, while Jefferson will always be associated with the doctrines of universal human rights that he wrote into the Declaration, thereby rendering it immortal, but this fine gentleman was in the spirit of *noblesse oblige,* not class warfare. Perhaps Samuel Adams may be regarded as a rabble-rouser, but he was no self-seeker, and demagogues were rare among the Signers.

A contrast is sometimes drawn between the men responsible for the Declaration and the framers of the Constitution, in the next decade, the former being described as radical and the latter as conservative. While there can be no question of the difference in mood in 1776 and 1787, or of the difference in circumstances, there does not appear to have been any sharp contrast between these two groups of men in terms of their economic status.

The average wealth of the Signers may actually have been greater than that of the framers of the Constitution. It was probably true in 1776, as John Adams said, that "several signed with regret, and several others with many doubts," but they all stood forth in this instance as champions of liberty. They were heralds of national independence and political self-government rather than class struggle and social revolution, and it is an ironical fact that a number of them suffered grievously in their own fortunes during the war and its aftermath.

After signing their names, some of them went into relative obscurity, leaving scarcely a trace behind. Most of them continued to perform public service as long as they could, and a few became major heroes of the young Republic. The first to die was John Morton of Pennsylvania, a plain farmer of Swedish stock; on July 2, 1776, he had cast one of the crucial votes that swung Pennsylvania to the side of independence.

The story is that some of his closest friends blamed him for this act, during the dark months that followed, and that on his deathbed he said: "Tell them that they will live to see the hour when they shall acknowledge it to have been the most glorious service that I ever rendered my country." This was in April, 1777, less than a year after his signing of the Declaration, and at that date it was still too early to say that the wisdom of his conduct had been proved conclusively.

The second to die was Button Gwinnett of Georgia, whose name actually comes first among the signatures, reading from the left. He fell in a duel in Savannah within a year, and his autograph is so rare that it has become almost priceless.

Of all the Signers, the one with the shortest life span was Thomas Lynch Jr., of South Carolina, who was sent to Congress in 1776 to take care of his stricken father and substitute for him, if necessary. He affixed his name to the engrossed document at the age of 27 and was lost at sea when 30. The longest-lived was the fabulous Charles Carroll of Carrollton, who emerged from obscurity in 1828 to participate in ceremonies marking the start of the Baltimore and Ohio Railroad, and lasted until 1832, dying at the age of ninety-five. He witnessed the dawn of the railroad era, but no other signer ever saw anything faster than a horse.

Our times are so different from the ones they knew that we cannot find in their words and actions specific solutions for our distinctive problems. As the author of the Declaration said, the earth belongs always to the living, not the dead. But, besides deserving remembrance for their own sakes as persons, they can teach us one supremely important lesson. In time of crisis, men of divergent opinions can stand together in the name of liberty, and prosperous men, as well as the less fortunate, can risk their lives and fortunes to advance that sacred cause.

Part 2

THE REVOLUTION'S CREATIVITY

COMMENTATORS OFTEN note that the conservatism of the American Revolution is in sharp contrast to the radicalism of the French and Russian Revolutions. Another distinction lies in the creativity of 1776 as opposed to the destructiveness of 1789 and 1917. The conservative American Revolution produced the most liberal kinds of documents, while the radical French and Russian Revolutions produced nothing to compare in quality and durability with the Declaration of Independence, the federal Constitution, and the Bill of Rights.

These three documents express American society's nature and goals, not merely for the eighteenth century but for our own time as well. As Julian P. Boyd remarks in the opening article of this section, the Declaration epitomizes the divergence between fear and faith that characterizes American life. Boyd views the Declaration as a statement of human rights, the meaning of which has expanded over the years. Jefferson posed an eloquent goal for all generations.

Another aspect of the Declaration, dealt with in Henry Steele

Commager's essay, is its effect outside the United States. As "a most subversive document," it has guided more than one revolution, in concept if not in substance. By this statement of revolutionary ideas, Americans "invented the mechanisms" that have continuously given life and meaning to dangerous doctrines. Thus the Declaration's impact, and consequently that of Jefferson, has been far-reaching.

Boyd returns to the Declaration's meaning for America in his discussion of Jefferson's reaffirmation of its principles in 1826. Undaunted by the nation's failure to fulfill these ideas totally, Jefferson firmly believed them viable. He found encouragement in American accomplishments and understood the difficulty of fully bridging reality and idealism. Jefferson belonged to a generation that willingly continued the struggle to attain what they believed valid and valuable.

Only in chronology is the federal Constitution second to the Declaration as a means of understanding American aspirations. Its compromises, concessions, and imperfections reflect American reality, just as the Declaration reflects American idealism. Those who gathered at Philadelphia in 1787 understood the difficult nature of their task, and they sought with courage and wisdom to find a solution to one of man's basic problems. Louis Nizer examines the rational approach taken in 1787 and finds within it parallels for problems facing the world. His expression of hope that all nations might with similar courage and wisdom solve their problems at San Francisco, as Americans did theirs at Philadelphia, was misplaced. In retrospect, however, the goal remains one toward which future generations must strive.

The federal Constitution was unfinished when the Philadelphia convention adjourned. Its authors understood that, and so too did its critics. The issue on which the opponents centered their attack was the absence of a Bill of Rights. A written guarantee of rights was an old American tradition, one which stemmed from the English Bill of Rights of 1688. Supporters of the Constitution quickly promised to remedy the deficiency in the first session of Congress under the new government. James Truslow

Adams discusses the Bill of Rights not as mere written words but as a spirit of the age which has been passed on to succeeding generations. Again, this document embodies aspirations which at times are honored more in the breach than in the observance. But the spirit of the Bill of Rights is pervasive and important, and, as Adams suggests, can only be kept alive by a constant rededication. Without a sense of renewal to these guarantees, regardless of how some may abuse them, all stand in danger of losing them.

In conclusion, Seelye Jones reflects on the incompleteness of the work of the Constitutional convention. The first Congress under the new Constitution had to flesh in the bare-bones structure devised at Philadelphia. Succeeding generations have continued to add to the Constitution on an ad hoc basis ever since, making the document vital, alive, and adaptable to the nation's changing needs.

The Great Decision by Which We Still Stand

by Julian P. Boyd

ON JULY 1, 1776, the members of the Continental Congress listened to the final hours of debate on Richard Henry Lee's motion to declare the united colonies an independent nation. The delegates from Massachusetts and Virginia sat impatiently as John Dickinson, representing the conservative point of view of the middle colonies, urged moderation, conciliation, and postponement. But the period of debate had long been over. Thomas Jefferson and the other members of the committee appointed to draw up a formal proclamation of nationhood were ready with their report.

All knew what the result of this closing moment of argument would be and few, if any, opinions were changed. Yet the right of discussion by representatives of the people was an important part of the great decision about to be taken and discussion was permitted to continue long after the issue was settled. "The Revolution," wrote John Adams, "was effected before the war

From the *New York Times Magazine*, July 1, 1945, copyright © 1945 by The New York Times Company.

commenced. The Revolution was in the hearts and minds of the people." But it is the nature of such an issue that only the future or discerning contemporaries such as Adams can understand this.

For the issue was not merely a question of separation from the British Empire. The Declaration of Independence as a secessionist document is a historic fact, a fact of momentous consequences to be sure, but a fact that was settled once for all on July 2, 1776, when the Lee motion was adopted. But the Declaration of Independence as an issue of human idealism is a never-ending conflict between attitudes of fear and attitudes of faith, between what is and what might be, between acquiescence and honorable daring.

As such, the Declaration of Independence means today precisely what it meant in 1776: the sovereign right of the people to overthrow, alter or abolish the forms of government under which they have lived and to establish new institutions in whatever form "to them shall seem most likely to effect their safety and happiness." The right of revolution is, of course, a dangerous right that is usually asserted in times, as Franklin put it, when "Passion governs, and she never governs wisely." Though it is called by other names and debated with other arguments, the issue is as much agitated today as it was in 1776. If the right decision today seems to be obscured by false counsel as well as by weighty arguments on both sides, consider what the responsible colonial had to face on the eve of the American Revolution.

"American independence," wrote the anonymous author of "Additions to Plain Truth, Addressed to the Inhabitants of America," "is as illusory, ruinous and impracticable as a liberal reconciliation with Great Britain is right, honorable and expedient." The author regarded himself as a realist, bent upon exposing to his well-meaning but deluded countrymen the true nature of the visionary, inflammatory utterances of Paine's "Common Sense." His words were read with approval and echoed vehemently in many a drawing room in Boston and Philadelphia and Charleston.

The newspaper and pamphlet press was filled with the same

dire warnings to Americans. The pulpit contributed some of its outstanding men to the side of established law and order, such as the Rev. Jonathan Boucher of Maryland and the Rev. John Joachim Zubly of Georgia. A young lady of one of the first families of Philadelphia voiced the same correct principles in her genteel and decorous journal. A Scottish lady of learning and undeniable charm, Janet Schaw, observing the mob-like acts of the Carolina patriots in intimidation of the Tidewater aristocrats, forgot her Scottish nationalism in the common danger to all believers in government by an élite.

Joseph Galloway, lawyer, wealthy citizen, friend of Benjamin Franklin, and one of the outstanding political figures of Pennsylvania, was alarmed at the lawless and riotous behavior of some of his countrymen who talked openly of independence and used all of his influence to persuade them to forsake a course that, to him, meant only ruin and destruction. Ambrose Serle, an Englishman who voiced both the official point of view and the conservative American position, could scarcely restrain himself when the Declaration of Independence was at last issued:

"The Congress have at length thought it convenient to throw off the mask. . . . A more impudent, false and atrocious Proclamation was never fabricated by the Hands of Man."

These were not irresponsible men and women. They and thousands of other sympathizers in America were, almost without exception, identified with the classes of society that claimed or accepted responsibility for governing. They were loyal, patriotic subjects of their sovereign, deeply concerned about the dangers into which their American compatriots were running.

Galloway, like many another of these loyal subjects, sacrificed his property, his profession, and even his family ties because of his fealty to the Crown and to convictions deeply rooted. These men did not need Mansfield and Blackstone to point out that revolution, despite the liberal tradition of 1688, was inimical to the British Constitution.

Though many of them were independent in mind and character, they were all affected in more or less degree by the subtly powerful forces of political and social orthodoxy—by education, by religion, by connections, and by the shining tradition of Anglo-Saxon experience in self-government. Independence to them was simply a denial of all authority and they regarded themselves as being, both by preference and by duty, among the guardians of authority.

Independence was not merely a species of disloyalty to the British sovereign, to whom most of the patriot leaders had sworn oaths of allegiance. It was treason as well to all that the crown symbolized—to the hard-won liberties of Englishmen, to the idea of constitutional government, to the ancient bonds that made America and England part of a great new world power.

Were not many British subjects taxed in their persons and goods without being represented in Parliament? Had not the power of England, scarcely a decade earlier, saved the weak and divided colonies from conquest by France? Had not the British Navy kept the seas open and safe for American commerce? Had not England, in the days of Raleigh, Frobisher, Cavendish and Drake and in competition with great Continental powers, established a firm foothold on the best area of North America and aided the colonies in reaching their present prosperous state? Did not the best reason and policy for the future dictate a firm strengthening of the harmonious ties between mother country and colonies?

Admittedly there were American rights to be claimed and grievances to be aired, but let them be stated and disposed of by constitutional means, not by the overthrow of law and order. The right of assembly, the right of appeal, the right of trial by a jury of peers—these were ancient British rights and no one could contravene them. If the present ministerial policies showed a spirit of vindictiveness or displayed a tendency to abuse American rights and privileges, let their wrongs be redressed by legal means already provided.

On the other hand, supposing the visionary, subversive and rebellious writings of Paine and others should be successful in persuading Americans to forswear their loyalty to the Crown and to the British Constitution—what then? Independence could be proclaimed, but could it be achieved?

Where was there an American Army to fight the British regulars? And where was there an American Navy to defend a thousand miles of coastline and to oppose the British Navy on the high seas? Since the defeat of the Spanish Armada two centuries earlier, no nation on earth had been able to match British seapower. Where were the resources to come from for conducting a war, assuming that the total American manpower could be put in the field? The colonies had been conceived and administered as sources of raw materials. There were few infant manufactures that could be counted upon to supply power, guns, equipment. Foreign credit would be needed to buy foreign goods. Would credit be supplied to a nation whose nationality was still only a rebellious hope?

To these loyal men and women the question was not open to debate, either as a question of political philosophy or as a question of political expediency. But when the colonists began to awaken to the fact that they were Americans, that they held in their hands immense potentialities, that as a free and untrammeled people they stood on the threshold of an infinite future, it did not matter much what logic or law opposed them. Their appeal was to a law higher than the British Constitution, though it took them twelve years to assume the ground they would ultimately have to stand on.

In their first reaction to stricter imperial control, the Americans asserted their rights as free-born British subjects. As the play of issues roused them anew, they asserted, as early as 1770, that their rights were American rights; that their legislatures were co-equal with the British Parliament; and that—foreshadowing the twentieth century—the empire was an association of equals, bound together by the Crown and its symbolic ties. Finally, they appealed to a law higher than man-made Constitutions, the law of nature and nature's God, by which they held indefeasible rights as men.

But it was too late for conciliatory proposals or for anyone to suggest putting the colonies on the same footing they were on in 1763. By the time the Coercive Acts of 1774 were enacted, three million people in America had been or were in process of being transported by a vision. Under the drive of this vision, amply sustained and extended by such firebrands as Samuel Adams and Patrick Henry, the colonial status of 1763 was no longer tolerable. Given this premise, it was only a logical progression from a demand for repeal of distasteful acts to a demand for an empire that would be in reality an association of equals, to a final demand for independent nationality.

If the colonies in these twelve years demanded more and more and assumed higher and higher ground in justification, it was less an evidence of a conspiracy to deceive than it was an evidence of the progressive awakening of the colonists to their new and overpowering vision—the vision of free-ranging commerce, of unexplored rivers and plains, of a surging and self-reliant people, of free institutions beckoning to the oppressed everywhere, of a puissant nation yet to be but fast coming within reach.

In the face of this powerful urge, latent since the planting of the first colony in Virginia, but now racing like heady wine through the veins of the colonists, the ministerial policies brought to Americans a sense of unity that had been quite impossible at Albany in 1754. There may have been some truth in the belief of British officialdom that eventual independence had always been the American purpose. But there was more truth in the view that Americans did not realize it themselves until realization was progressively forced upon them by imperial policy after 1763. The beginnings of a sense of American nationality owe perhaps as much to George Townshend and Lord North as to Samuel Adams and Thomas Paine.

Thoughtful Americans such as Jefferson, Washington, Wythe and Franklin still hesitated until the winter of 1775 and then, as Jefferson wrote, "a phrenzy of revenge seems to have seized all ranks of people."

It was too late to dismiss the vision—and with it the danger to Britain—as the work of a few agitators such as Thomas Paine, Samuel Adams and Patrick Henry. Men of substance and position were aroused as well as the rank and file. Wilson, Jefferson and Adams could argue learnedly in their pamphlets about the true nature of the British Constitution and could state the philosophical justification for American rights as ably as it could be stated. But the concept of government by consent of the governed was intelligible as well to artisans, farmers, merchants, frontiersmen, traders and seamen. What the rank and file lacked in knowledge of the philosophy of government they made up in passionate defense of their convictions. "Common Sense" fell upon fertile soil in January, 1776.

Under Pitt, England had also caught a vision, a vision of a new Roman Empire. Ironically, the new strength and purpose given to England by Pitt helped to awaken in Americans their own interpretation of this vision. "The foundations of the future grandeur and stability of the British Empire lie in America," wrote Franklin in 1760, "and though, like other foundations, they are low and little seen, they are, nevertheless, broad and strong enough to support the greatest political structure human wisdom ever yet erected."

This interpretation of the sweep of empire was echoed in 1776 in Jefferson's first draft of the Declaration of Independence: "We might have been a free and great people together; but a communication of grandeur and of freedom it seems is below their dignity. Be it so, since they will have it: the road to glory and happiness is open to us too; we will climb it in a separate State."

Never before had Americans, or any people, faced so momentous an issue. It would seem, at this distance, to have been easy to confuse the minds of the people and to make them hesitate more than they did about denying the authority of their sworn sovereign. The course they were set upon might lead to a gallows or at the least to loss of property and privileges. Or it might lead to a new kind of nation, a nation that, conscious of its purpose and its strength, could become the hope of the world.

Never had a few hundred thousand men held in their hands an answer that demanded so much courage or wisdom of fortitude

—or one that so greatly affected the lives of hundreds of millions in the future. There were some among them who were influenced in their course by smuggling, land-hunger, debts, fisheries and other material factors. But here was an ancient human hope, stirring in the hearts of men as it never had before, ready to be proclaimed and to be given a broad new land in which to flourish. Their choice, incomprehensible to thousands of their fellow Americans who chose rather to abide by loyalties of the past than to run after visions of the future, was made as became men of honor and integrity—not as irresponsible radicals or agitators, but as men defending human rights.

A purpose so exalted demanded a solemn affirmation worthy of the moment and of the future. Here is that affirmation as Jefferson first drafted it:

"When in the course of human events it becomes necessary for a people to advance from that subordination in which they have hitherto remained, and to assume among the powers of the earth the equal & independent station to which the laws of nature and of nature's god entitle them, a decent respect to the opinions of mankind requires that they should declare the causes which impel them to the change.

"We hold these truths to be sacred & undeniable; that all men are created equal & independent, that from that equal creation they derive rights inherent & inalienable, among which are the preservation of life, & liberty & the pursuit of happiness; that to secure these ends, governments are instituted among them, deriving their just powers from the consent of the governed; that whenever any form of government shall become destructive of these ends, it is the right of the people to alter or to abolish it, & to institute new government, laying its foundation on such principles & organizing its powers in such form as to them shall seem most likely to effect their safety & happiness."

It was an observant and liberal Englishman, Dr. Richard Price, who wrote at the conclusion of the American Revolution: "Perhaps I do not go too far when I say, next to the introduction of

Christianity among mankind, the American revolution many prove the most important step in the progressive course of human improvement."

The importance of the purpose stated so exaltedly in the Declaration and defended so heroically by men under Washington derives not merely from the fact that it was asserted in 1776 by a band of determined patriots. It derives also from the fact that it must perpetually be restated and redefended. The importance of the Declaration of Independence is that it must always be declared and defended against those counterparts of Ambrose Serle in every generation who think its meaning "impudent, false, and atrocious."

Our Declaration Is Still a Rallying Cry

by Henry Steele Commager

THE UNITED STATES was born of rebellion and grew to greatness through revolution. No other nation, it is safe to say, has a revolutionary history that is so long or so comprehensive, and no other has a record that is so subversive.

Certainly the Declaration of Independence has some claim to be considered the most subversive document in modern history, and members of the Daughters of the American Revolution and the John Birch Society and all the other organizations that mortally fear revolution would do well to work to bar it from schools and public libraries. For, consider how explosive are its principles, if they are to be taken seriously: all men are created equal; all have a right to life, liberty and the pursuit of happiness; the purpose of government is to secure *these* rights; men have a right to overthrow existing governments and to make new governments!

Americans did not invent these heady doctrines, but they did something far more dangerous; they invented the mechanisms which gave them life and meaning. In the words of John Adams

From the *New York Times Magazine,* July 2, 1961, copyright © 1961 by The New York Times Company.

they *"realized* the doctrines of the wisest writers." Thus, while philosophers had long asserted that men make government, it remained for the Americans to contrive that fundamental democratic institution whereby men can, in fact, create a government, the constitutional convention. Thus, while philosophers had long argued that all power was limited and that no government could exercise unlimited power, it remained for Americans to devise really effective legal limitations on government: written constitutions, checks and balances, dual federalism, judicial review—devices that for the first time in history really limited government.

But the Declaration was just a beginning of the revolution. Thereafter the United States embarked upon a career that was deeply subversive of most of the things governments and rulers in the Old World believed in and stood for. Just think: no established church, no royalty, no hereditary nobility, no military establishment, no great vested interests, no colonies to exploit. And—to look at its positive features—self-government, limited government, religious freedom, popular education, and a classless society.

The more we contemplate the American experience the more we are impressed by its deeply revolutionary character. No wonder that when the perspicacious Tocqueville came to America in the mid-Eighteen Thirties he could report, in effect, "I have seen the future, and it works!"—and go home to warn France, and all Europe, to prepare for an inevitable revolution along American lines. "The question here discussed," he said—and he was talking about equality in America—"is interesting not only to the United States, but to the whole world; it concerns not a nation, but all mankind." That was something that thoughtful Americans and Europeans realized from the beginning—that the experience of America concerned not just a nation but all mankind.

Americans were the first people to revolt against a mother country and set up on their own. This established a pattern, first for the nations of Latin America, and eventually for nations and peoples in the Old World and in ancient continents. The revolts against colonialism which have swept Asia and Africa in our own time have their historical antecedents or beginnings in American experience. If any people should sympathize with the impulse to "dissolve the political bands which have connected them with another, and to assume . . . separate and equal station," it is Americans, for in a very real sense they initiated and inspired it.

The United States was the first nation founded squarely on the right of revolution; on the "right to alter or abolish" government. That principle is to be found not only in the Declaration, but in the institution of the constitutional convention. What Madison said shortly after the inauguration of the new government is true today:

"If there be a principle that ought not to be questioned within the United States, it is that every nation has a right to abolish an old government and establish a new one. This principle is not only recorded in every public archive, written in every American heart, and sealed with the blood of a host of American martyrs, but is the only lawful tenure by which the United States hold their existence as a nation."

The United States was the first nation to embark upon the experiment of a broad, popular self-government. Government, said Jefferson, derives its powers from the consent of the governed. The government embraced the whole body politic, and consent meant something more than acquiescence; it meant participation. It is fashionable, now, in some quarters, to recall that suffrage was limited in eighteenth-century America, and to quote anguished criticisms of democracy from the rich and the well-born. What is important is that incomparably more people participated in the daily business of government in the American states than anywhere else in the world; that limitations on suffrage evaporated with an ease that astonished envious European liberals; that there would have been no occasion for complaints against democracy if democracy had not been a very real thing; and that, after all, the Federalists did go under in 1800 and the Jeffersonians, with faith in the ability of men to govern themselves, did triumph.

Americans were pioneers in self-government. As Tom Paine

wrote: "America made a stand, not for herself only, but for the world, and looked beyond the advantages which she could receive." She undertook to prove to the rest of mankind that self-government could work. All through the nineteenth century upperclass visitors reported that it did not work, but in that same century some twenty million emigrants from the Old World to the New gave America a resounding vote of confidence.

Americans were the first people deliberately to create a nation: what Lincoln said at Gettysburg was literally true, that our forefathers had "brought forth a new nation." Theretofore nations had not been created; they had grown out of century-long historical processes: thus England, France, Denmark, Spain and many others. But American nationalism was a creative act, a product of the deliberate application of will and intelligence by statesmen, soldiers, scholars, men of letters, artists, scientists and others of all ranks to the task of nation-making.

Where, in Old World countries, the foundations of nationalism were laid long before the political superstructure was erected, in the United States the "Founding Fathers" first built the political structure, and thereafter filled in the rest. They contrived the constitutional mechanisms, the political practices, exploited the economic bases, developed the social resources, and added, for good measure, the historical and the cultural ingredients as well.

With this unprecedented experience with nationalism Americans should have the liveliest sympathy for those peoples throughout the globe who are today striving to create a nation. We were the first to show that it could be done and we should be the first to welcome others when they try to repeat our experience.

The first of the truths which Jefferson announced as "self-evident" was the truth that all men are created equal. We will not inquire, here, just what Jefferson meant by the elusive term; its significance—as with most of the great phrases of history—is not descriptive but prophetic. What the phrase came to mean was never better put than by Lincoln in his Springfield speech of 1857.

The Fathers, he said, meant to set up "a standard maxim for free society, which should be familiar to all, and revered by all; constantly looked to, constantly labored for, and even though never perfectly attained, constantly approximated, and thereby constantly spreading and deepening its influence and augmenting the happiness and value of life to all people of all colors everywhere * * * Its authors meant it [the Declaration] to be * * * a stumbling block to those who in after times might seek to turn a free people back into the hateful paths of despotism."

The concept of equality, first announced as a general principle in the Declaration of Independence, has worked like a ferment in American society, and in the American mind—and not in America alone. Each successive generation of Americans has, in its own way, felt called on to square reality with the principle of equality.

"Created equal." It applied to the political processes, and struck down limitations on the suffrage for men and eventually for women. It applied to the social process and challenged every manifestation of class—challenged though it could not prevent slavery; challenged though it did not prevent the continuing assertion of white supremacy after slavery was gone; and in the end forced Americans to resolve the pernicious dilemma that had so long frustrated them.

It applied to the economy and helped create an open economic order where material well-being came to be assumed both as a proper foundation to equality, and as a right. It applied to religion and made impossible not only an established church but the association of any one church with social or political power. It applied to education and eventually required an equal chance at education for all comers—a requirement only now in process of realization.

Political equality is now a reality throughout most of the free world. Social equality has been realized in many countries; economic equality has not yet been attained in large parts of the globe. Who can doubt that Tocqueville was right when he predicted that the principles and practices of equality that he found illustrated in America would spread to the Old World, and beyond?

We have two obvious responsibilities here. The first is to put an end to the shameful inequalities that persist in our society. Inequality—as Lincoln said of slavery itself—"deprives our republican example of its just influence in the world; enables the enemies of free institutions with plausibility to taunt us as hypocrites; causes the real friends of freedom to doubt our sincerity; and forces so many good men among ourselves into an open war with the very fundamental principles of civil liberty * * *." The second responsibility is to welcome and support those political practices and economic developments that promise a greater degree of equality in other lands.

Americans were the first people who took for granted and exploited the possibilities of change. Though the eighteenth century did embrace the notion of progress, that progress was, on the whole, an abstraction rather than a reality. It was something that would take place over the centuries, and it was tempered by the conviction that though material circumstances might change, human nature itself would not really change. Americans were the first to prove that, given favorable economic conditions and a favorable political climate, progress would be immensely accelerated, and that human nature itself could be changed in a single generation.

Men *could* throw off the shackles of the past; they *could* emancipate themselves from tyranny and ignorance and poverty; they *could* lift themselves by their own bootstraps. Just give them a chance! Let them enjoy freedom; let them govern themselves; give them an education; provide them with land and with jobs; let them worship as they wished—and think as they wished; assure them of equality; give them a chance. Then, not centuries or millennia, but a few years would suffice for progress.

That is what Jefferson said, again and again. That is what the Declaration of Independence said, with its emphasis on equality and on the pursuit of happiness. And that is what Jefferson returned to in his last public letter—a letter celebrating the fiftieth anniversary of that Declaration of Independence which he had penned:

"May it be to the world, what I believe it will be, * * * the signal for arousing men to burst the chains under which monkish ignorance and superstition had persuaded them to bind themselves, and to assume the blessings and security of self-government * * *. All eyes are opened, or opening, to the rights of man. The general spread of the light of science has already laid open to every view the palpable truth that the mass of mankind has not been born with saddles on their backs, nor a favored few booted and spurred, ready to ride them legitimately * * *. There are grounds of hope for others * * *."

Of all peoples, then, we should be most ready to sympathize with those who are trying to close the desperate gap between what they are, and what they might be; who are trying to catch up in one generation with the progress of centuries.

The methods of this global revolution, too, are familiar enough. For it is one of the great paradoxes of history that the revolt of Asia and Africa against the "West" is being carried on with the tools and techniques devised by the West. The political instrument is Western nationalism; the social instrument is Western equality; the economic instrument is Western science and technology.

Now, while the Industrial Revolution had its origins in Europe, nowhere were natural resources, abundant labor, technical and scientific skills more happily combined to lift the general level of well-being than in the United States. Ours, it has been observed, is a business civilization; it would be more accurate to call it a technological civilization. Conservative business men who never tire of pointing out the immense achievements of American technology should be the first to sympathize with the impoverished millions of Asia and Africa who have learned the lesson that America taught: that it is possible to lift the level of a society by the application of science and technology.

There is one final consideration that is relevant. The colonies, said Jefferson "are, and *of right ought to be,* free." That was a phrase which echoes again and again in the speeches, letters and public papers of the time—of right *ought to be.* If colonies were not represented, they ought to be; if religion was not free, it ought to be; if men were not free, they ought to be. That "ought to be" was a rallying cry, a call to duty and to war. It took for granted that man and Providence would work together to achieve ends that were right and just.

Should we not say today, that men everywhere ought to be free; that they ought to be independent; that they ought to enjoy equality; that they ought to share in a higher standard of living and in the pursuit of happiness?

The Declaration of Independence is not merely a museum piece. It is not a parchment to take out once a year, celebrate with ceremonial reverence, and then return to the sterility of a glass case. It is not merely a historical document, something to learn in school as we learn so many things that we promptly forget. It is vital and immediate. It argues a case that is still valid and announces principles that are still true. It still calls upon us to pledge our lives, our fortunes and our honor to their vindication.

Jefferson's Final
Testament of Faith

by Julian P. Boyd

ON JUNE 21, 1826, the aged statesman at Monticello made the next to the last entry in his register of letters received, a register begun nearly half a century earlier and, since 1790, kept up to date with thoroughgoing completeness. The entry which thus brought to a close an inventory of what has been called the greatest treasure house of information ever left by a single man read: "Weightman R. C. Mayor Washn. June 16. [invitn]."

In the adjoining column of out-letters there is no entry under June 24 for Jefferson's reply. The omission is eloquent. Three other letters written that day are recorded, but the one which stood apart from these ordinary communications, distinguished by its nobly worded affirmation, was too closely identified with the purpose of a dedicated life to be remembered.

The vision and faith of the elder statesman submerged the systematic habit of the clerk. The letter had no need to be recorded in such a register. It was a farewell address affirming an unshaken confidence in the capacity of the people for self-government, and history would record it in the minds and hearts of those for whom it was intended. Posted to Mayor Weightman of Washington, it was really addressed to the people of America and of the world.

The copy of the letter that Mayor Weightman received was read at the celebration held in Washington, July 4, 1826, and was immediately published, along with letters by the two other surviving signers of the Declaration of Independence and by two former Presidents, James Madison and James Monroe. But the undated, unsigned rough draft of Jefferson's famous letter has never been reproduced. It has been recently identified among the large body of Jefferson manuscripts in the Massachusetts Historical Society. "Scored and scratched like a schoolboy's exercise" —as was said of the rough draft of the Declaration itself—Jefferson's original composition of this letter presents a final glimpse of his life-long habit of striving for the right word and the felicitous phrase. The unsteady hand, the economy of words, even the unusual employment of abbreviations ("f. c." for "fellow citizens," a device rarely if ever used by Jefferson elsewhere) give a more poignant meaning to this expression of an unfaltering faith, uttered at what cost of effort and pain we can only guess. But we may be certain that this painfully wrought letter represented a final summoning of swiftly departing strength.

Mayor Weightman's "invitn" was respectful, polite and stereotyped:

> Sir, As chairman of the committee appointed by the citizens of Washington to make arrangements for celebrating the fiftieth anniversary of American Independence in a manner worthy of the Metropolis of the nation, I am directed to invite you, as one of the signers of the ever-memorable Declaration of the 4th of July 1776, to honor the city with your presence on the occasion. I am further instructed to inform you that, on receiving your acceptance of this invitation, a

special deputation will be sent to accompany you from your residence to this city and back again to your home. With sentiments of the highest respect and veneration, I have the honor to be, your most obedient servant,

R. S. WEIGHTMAN,

Mayor of Washington and Chairman of the Committee of Arrangements.

The letter, as Jefferson would have recognized instantly, betrayed its impersonal character. The phrase "as one of the signers" was evidence enough. So phrased, the letter could also be dispatched to John Adams at Quincy and to Charles Carroll of Carrollton, the other surviving signers. Sensitive to a high degree and proud of his authorship of the statement of a people's ideals, Jefferson must have noted that he was not addressed as the author of that immortal document.

He must have understood also. Mayor Weightman was a busy man; the chairman of a committee on arrangements is always busy. There were matters of protocol to be attended to; political nuances to be borne in mind; illuminations, fireworks, decorations, banquets, parades and police details to be arranged; schedules to be drawn up and coordinated (though the word would not assume its full stature in such a context for another century); selection of orators, careful wording of toasts and responses to toasts. (In a few years a boldly worded toast would have the power and effect of a Presidential proclamation.)

But the important matter was not the question of authorship but the Declaration itself. How could it be celebrated worthily? Could fireworks and illuminations and oratory bring about understanding? Who, indeed, could understand the zeal and the vision that had aroused and united a people? Who even knew or remembered all that had taken place? For years Jefferson and John Adams had been writing letters about this great subject. Even they, in this incomparable exchange of philosophical reflections on its meaning, could not always agree as to what had happened, nor explore to their satisfaction the complex origins or the probable destinies of an ideal.

What was being celebrated was not a document, certainly not the act of drafting it, not military valor or brilliance, not altogether the establishment of a nation. The orators of the day would inevitably allude to all of these, paying their tributes in periods of classic structure. But these were reflections of the inward event, not the event itself. In the final analysis—at least as Jefferson understood it—what they were celebrating was an idea, an idea so simple, so consonant with justice and morality, so powerful in the strength it released, that all manner of people, great and small, high and low, rich and poor, had understood it and responded to it: the idea that everything rested upon and within the individual human being; that each individual possessed within himself something sacred and inviolable; that no government, group, or authority in any form or in any sphere of society could encroach upon that sacred core of right, save by consent of the individual.

It was the people's understanding and their response to this concept that had brought forth the Declaration of Independence, had established a government, had enabled them to carry through a long and difficult war.

A worthy celebration of the political birth of such an ideal would be to live by its tenets. Fanfare and oratory could not do harm, but neither could they bring understanding or progress. Paying tribute, they might possibly obscure unwelcome truth, drawing a tinsel veil over the rift between ideal and actuality. The great question was whether the rift had grown greater or less since 1776. Most important of all, was there ground for hoping, after fifty years of experience, that it would diminish in the future?

If Jefferson, pondering the letter of the chairman of the committee on arrangements, turned his thoughts back to the events of 1776, he must have reflected that a chasm between ideal and actuality had also existed then. Many who had shouted for

Liberty had voted for authority. He may have remembered that pamphlet published shortly before he arrived in Philadelphia in May, 1776. It was signed "A Native of the Colony," but all knew its author to be Carter Braxton, aristocratic planter from the Virginia Tidewater.

Braxton, a man of probity and a respected leader, talked of Liberty but meant status quo. Establish independence, he had advised, but in creating your new institutions copy the British Constitution. Copy especially its frank acknowledgment of the necessity of a ruling class. Virginia had long been governed by such a class. She had developed an incomparable group of statesmen, conscious of their privilege but conscious also of their responsibility for governing and trained from youth with that end in view. Was it not a good system? Had it not worked? What other society, except perhaps in the age of Pericles or of Elizabeth, had given to the world at one time such men devoted to the public weal as the Lees, the Randolphs, Washington, Pendleton, Jefferson, Mason, Wythe, Taylor, Henry, Marshall, Madison, and a dozen others of the first rank? Had they not been produced by an aristocratic society?

This was an old theme even in 1776 and no Declaration would diminish the ranks of those who uttered it. Patrick Henry had called Braxton's advice "silly"; John Adams called it "absurd"; Richard Henry Lee called it "contemptible." Jefferson did not waste time in name-calling. He may have remembered how, two days after he had arrived in Philadelphia, he had written the letter which might have deprived him of the opportunity to write the Declaration of Independence. "Should our Convention propose to establish now a form of government," he wrote to Thomas Nelson, "perhaps it might be agreeable to recall for a short time their delegates. * * * In truth, it is the whole object of the present controversy; for should a bad government be instituted for us in future it had been as well to have accepted at first the bad one offered to us beyond the water without the risk and expence of contest."

But he did more than advance this delicate hint. Performing his full share of Congressional chores, he nevertheless sought to relieve his anxiety about Virginia's new government by drafting a Constitution himself. Only then, having done his utmost under the circumstances to bring his voice to bear upon the "whole object," did he turn to the responsibility that Congress had laid upon him for drafting a justification to the world of the act of independence.

He must have remembered how his great law teacher and colleague, George Wythe, arrived too late with his proposed Constitution. The convention at Williamsburg had already revised and modified to the point of unrecognizability the plan that George Mason had laid before it and had worn itself out with a multiplicity of other business.

Besides, Jefferson's plan was too radical. It extended the suffrage far beyond its old limits. It equalized representation in the Legislature and therefore threatened the dominance of the Tidewater planters. It stipulated that anyone who wanted land could have up to fifty acres. It threatened privilege at the same time that it opened up new avenues and opportunities for those not of the ruling class. The convention, borrowing his preamble, tacked on its own version of a safe and sound government: little or no change in representation, in suffrage, in the all-important system of county government. In brief, a constitution fitted to Virginia as she was, not to Virginia as she might be.

This was one of the chief reasons why, during that arduous summer as he labored amid the multitude of Congressional duties and anxieties, his eyes were constantly turned toward Virginia. Serving on more than a score of committees, drafting the Declaration of Independence and many reports and resolutions, sitting day after day on an investigating committee and taking pages of notes of testimony about the misfortunes of the Army in Canada, he had performed a prodigious amount of work in Congress. Yet he was torn by anxiety to return home and to engage in the great work of reforming the new commonwealth according to the principles of a republic.

He may have remembered how desperately, late in July, 1776, he had appealed to Richard Henry Lee to come to Philadelphia and relieve him in order that he might return to his ill wife in Virginia and to "the whole object"—"for God's sake, for your country's sake, and for my sake, come." Never, then or later, did he lose sight of the cause of the Union and its identity with the cause of liberty, but in this critical year of 1776 he knew that the foundations must be laid in the states.

He also may have remembered how, on returning, he had faced a desperate dilemma in the autumn of 1776. He had gone back to Williamsburg to reform by law what he had failed to accomplish in his constitution. He had scarcely begun when a dispatch rider from President Hancock brought him news of his appointment as Minister to France. For three days he had kept the rider waiting. Without French aid how could the colonies triumph? But what object was there in triumph if the ideal to which the nation was committed should be frustrated by clinging to the old order? His decision had been firm. Refusing the appointment, he had plunged at once into legislation, drafting and presenting bill after bill, all based on his understanding of the ideal toward which the people were aiming.

A bill to abolish entail and primogeniture, twin pillars of an aristocratic order. Five bills to set up courts of law. A bill to exempt dissenters from paying taxes to an established church. A bill for the naturalization of foreigners—*all* foreigners, not simply foreigner Protestants, as many would have it. A bill to revise the laws, the entire system of laws, not merely a few. A bill to establish auditors of public accounts. A bill to remove the seat of government from the center of the plantation aristocracy nearer to the center of population. Some of these were already famous.

But would the orators of the day know about the bill to divide Fincastle County? If they only knew that, they would know what the phrases of the Declaration of Independence really meant. How could they be expected to know about Fincastle County? Even its name had disappeared in 1776 and the issue that it brought forth had been fought out in a committee that kept no minutes. How could an orator apostrophize something so prosaic, so lacking in epic grandeur as a bill to divide a county? It could be done, of course, if only the orators and historians knew what had taken place in committee and if nearer the truth, the title of the bill had read:

"A bill to prevent land-capitalists from engrossing millions of acres that belong to the commonwealth; to forestall their exploiting settlers by charging exorbitant prices; to break up their alliance with the aristocratic planters; to keep these two powerful groups from manipulating government for their own ends; to open up the Western wilderness for settlers who would establish homes and schools and churches, not for the profit of absentee capitalists; to limit the size of any one man's holdings of land; to equalize representation so that the more numerous small farmers of the West would have a voice in government equal to that of the small ruling class in the East, and for other purposes."

The bill to divide Fincastle County does not read in these terms as printed in the statute books. But these were the issues on which it hinged in committee debates and there the author of the Declaration of Independence spoke for the application of its ideals to the business at hand. Twice he had thwarted Carter Braxton; twice he had taken charge of bills that Braxton had sponsored; twice he had remolded them to suit the just and fair objects he had in view.

The "True and Absolute Proprietors" of several million acres of land in Fincastle County (better known as Kentucky) could never again dream of an independent proprietary government in that region. Behind the committee doors the author of the Declaration of Independence had won in a struggle with powerful forces; but his weapon was stronger—it was the idea that there are certain truths all men hold to be self-evident.

Jefferson may have wondered, reading Mayor Weightman's invitation, whether the nation considered these truths as self-evident in 1826 as it had in 1776. He would be spared the blast of another orator in mid-century who would call the phrases of the Declaration "glittering generalities." But there were signs at hand that read the same way. His generation had spoken openly and vigorously in behalf of freedom for slaves, differing only in methods proposed. No leader could now advocate such ideas and expect to remain a leader.

There were other signs that spelled disillusionment. But beyond these there was something else to be discerned. Preoccupied though they might be with commerce, finance and material rewards, the people were resourceful, inventive, aggressive; their faces betrayed a sublime self-confidence. Such confidence, irresistibly carrying the people westward across the mountains and into the great valley, was not inspired by the ideas held forth by the Carter Braxtons of the land. Such confidence may not have been produced by the assertion of self-evident truths, but the assertion harmonized with the fact and gave it meaning. When the vital test came, as it surely would in countless other Fincastle County struggles, the assertion would remain an inexhaustible arsenal.

The faith remained firm, but Jefferson's hand had the tremor of age as he wrote his reply to Mayor Weightman's invitation. Half a century earlier he had used a scrap of the Declaration to write down the dimensions of a horse stall; to rebuke a general who thought more of military rank than of his country; to draft a Congressional report. Paper was now plentiful, but, devoid of the prodigal habits that characterized his countrymen, he could not abandon an old custom. Yet the paper he used to draw up his shaky, crossed-out, and interlined letter to Mayor Weightman was less a scrap than a symbol. It was the address leaf of a letter he had received from a brilliant young Hollander, Adrian van der Kemp, who had come to America because of the flame that had been kindled in 1776. Few had been so brilliant and so devoted to a cause as van der Kemp, but there had been countless others who also had come because of "an instrument pregnant with our own and the fate of the world."

His final testament of faith was brief, for he was ill and feeble.
But he drafted it slowly and carefully and then copied it fair:

> Monticello June 24, 26
> Respected Sir
> The kind invitation I receive from you on the part of the
> citizens of the city of Washington, to be present with them
> at their celebration of the 50th anniversary of American
> independence; as one of the surviving signers of the instru-
> ment, pregnant with our own, and the fate of the world,
> is most flattering to myself, and heightened by the honorable
> accompaniment proposed for the comfort of such a journey.
> it adds sensibly to the sufferings of sickness, to be deprived
> by it of a personal participation in the rejoicings of that day.
> but acquiescence is a duty, under circumstances not placed
> among those we are permitted to controul. I should indeed,
> with peculiar delight, have met and exchanged there, con-
> gratulations personally, with the small band, the remnant
> of that host of worthies, who joined with us, on that day,
> in the bold and doubtful election we were to make, for our
> country, between submission, or the sword; and to have
> enjoyed with them the consolatory fact that our fellow
> citizens, after half a century of experience and prosperity,
> continue to approve the choice we made. may it be to the
> world what I believe it will be, (to some parts sooner, to
> others later, but finally to all,) the Signal of arousing men
> to burst the chains, under which Monkish ignorance and
> superstition had persuaded them to bind themselves, and
> to assume the blessings & security of self government. the
> form which we have substituted restores the free right to the
> unbounded exercise of reason and freedom of opinion. all
> eyes are opened, or opening to the rights of man. the
> general spread of the light of science has already laid open
> to every view the palpable truth that the mass of mankind
> has not been born, with saddles on their backs, nor a favored
> few booted and spurred, ready to ride them legitimately, by

the grace of god, these are grounds of hope for others. for [our] selves let the annual return of this day, for ever refresh our recollections of these ri[ghts] and an undiminished devotion to them.

[I wi]ll ask permission here to express the pleasure with which [I sh]ould have met my ancient neighbors of the City of Washington and it's vicinities, with whom I passed so many years of a pleasing social intercourse; an intercourse which so much relieved the anxieties of the public cares, and left impressions so deeply engraved in my affections, as never to be forgotten. with my regret that ill health forbids me the gratification of an acceptance, be pleased to receive for yourself and those for whom you write the assurance of my highest respect and friendly attachments.

Th: Jefferson

The day the orators spoke was his and Adams' last, but the words of Adams that the historians have doubted remain perpetually true: "Jefferson still survives."

Our Founding Fathers at San Francisco

by Louis Nizer

AS THE San Francisco Conference gets under way, America may well indulge in the national tradition of turning to her founding statesmen for wisdom and inspiration. Americans are too independent-minded to be fettered by mere precedent, but they recognize their comparative inexperience in world affairs and they respect profoundly the minds of the constitutional fathers. The debate which has arisen over the Dumbarton Oaks proposals, including the Yalta agreements, resembles so much the conflicts in our own early American history that we may draw comfort from the parallel.

I point to the past only because we are now offered the opportunity, from a perspective achieved through the passing of a century and a half, to test the wisdom of those events and thus to obtain a practical guide for the present.

First, our forefathers drew the Articles of Confederation. It took three years before they were adopted. Thereafter, for six years our States struggled to make these Articles effective. They failed, because the Articles of Confederation overzealously guarded the sovereignty of States.

From the *New York Times Magazine,* April 29, 1945, copyright © 1945 by The New York Times Company.

Article II provided: "Each State retains its sovereignty, freedom and independence." Each State had one vote and it was necessary that nine out of thirteen States should approve any measure. There was no power to levy or collect taxes or to raise an army. There was only the power to recommend that the States make their contributions in these respects. Consequently taxes could not be collected and an army could not be organized. No amendment to the Articles was possible without a unanimous vote.

Finally, in 1787, the Articles were abandoned and the Constitution was proposed. Similarly in modern history, the League of Nations having failed, we are considering a new organization at San Francisco.

When the Constitution was first drafted it constituted a new and radical approach. The powers of the States were compromised in the interest of "international" peace among the thirteen States. But the same problems which plague us today did so then. For example, what was the relationship to be between large and small States? Madison wrote:

> To the difficulties already mentioned may be added the interfering pretensions of the larger and smaller States. * * * We may well suppose that neither side would entirely yield to the other, and consequently that the struggle could be terminated only by compromise * * * and as far as either of them is well founded, it shows that the convention must have been compelled to sacrifice theoretical propriety to the force of extraneous considerations. (The Federalist, No. 39.)

In the same way today, San Francisco is being asked to recognize the reality of power as against the "theoretical propriety" of equality of small States. As Winston Churchill said on March 15, 1945:

> We may deplore if we choose that there is a difference between the great and the small, between the strong and the weak in the world. There is undoubtedly such a difference and it would be foolish to upset the good arrangements

proceeding on a broad front for the sake of trying to attain immediately to what is a hopeless ideal.

Similarly the disappointment of any nation because its view concerning Poland, for example, has not been adopted, should be tempered by the realization that world peace is not attained by abstract justice, but by agreement among the great powers upon an approximation of justice. Once more we can turn to our own past statesmen. When George Washington sent the final draft of the Constitution to Congress, he accompanied it with a letter in which he wrote these classic words:

> That it will meet the full and entire approbation of every State is not perhaps to be expected; but each will doubtless consider, that had her interest alone been consulted, the consequences might have been particularly disagreeable or injurious to others; that it is liable to as few exceptions as could reasonably have been expected, we hope and believe; that it may promote the lasting welfare of that country so dear to us all, and secure her freedom and happiness, is our most ardent wish.

Many distinguished men of that period saw serious imperfections in the Constitution which today we are inclined to believe was an inspired document. But the great men of that era sought first to adopt the Constitution, relying upon evolutionary processes to correct the errors. They feared that delays and debates upon every point would divide the thirteen States and prevent the growth of the nation. It is well to remember now that Jefferson said about the United States Constitution:

> There are indeed some faults which revolted me a good deal in the first moment; but we must be contented to travel on toward perfection step by step * * *. We must be contented with the ground which this Constitution will gain for us and hope that a favorable moment will come for correcting what is amiss in it.

Those who clamor for perfection now with respect to Dumbarton Oaks and the voting agreements will think that Alexander

Hamilton is speaking to them when he wrote about the Constitution:

> Concessions on the part of friends of the plan, that it has not a claim to absolute perfection, have afforded matter of no small triumph to its enemies. "Why," say they, "should we adopt an imperfect thing? Why not amend it and make it perfect before it is irrevocably established?" This may be plausible enough, but it is only plausible. In the first place I remark that the extent of these concessions has been greatly exaggerated. They have been stated as amounting to an admission that the plan is radically defective, and that without material alterations the rights and the interests of the community cannot be safely confided to it. This, as far as I have understood the meaning of those who make the concessions, is an entire perversion of their sense. No advocate of the measure can be found who will not declare as his sentiment that the system, though it may not be perfect in every part, is upon the whole a good one; is the best that the present views and circumstances of the country will permit; and is such a one as promises every species of security which a reasonable people can desire.
>
> I answer in the next place, that I should esteem it the extreme of imprudence to prolong the precarious state of our national affairs, and to expose the Union to the jeopardy of successive experiments, in the chimerical pursuit of a perfect plan. I never expect to see a perfect work from imperfect man. The result of the deliberations of all collective bodies must necessarily be a compound as well of the errors and prejudices, as of the good sense and wisdom of the individuals of whom they are composed. The compacts which are to embrace thirteen distinct States in a comn. n bond of amity and union, must as necessarily be a compromise of as many dissimilar interests and inclinations. (The Federalist, No. 85.)

James Madison called the Constitution a "bundle of compromises * * * a mosaic of second choices accepted in the interest of union" and Benjamin Franklin felicitiously telescoped the entire debate of that day, and for that matter of this day, when he said:

> I confess that there are several parts of this Constitution which I do not at present approve, but I am not sure that I shall never approve them * * *. I doubt, too, whether any other convention we can obtain may be able to make a better Constitution. For when you assemble a number of men to have the advantage of their joint wisdom, you inevitably assemble with those men all their prejudices, their passions, their errors of opinion, their local interests and their selfish views. From such an assembly can a perfect production be expected? Thus I consent, sir, to this Constitution because I expect no better and because I am not sure it is not the best. The opinion I have had of its errors I sacrifice to the public good.

It is not unlikely that the imperfect achievements at San Francisco may some day be regarded with the same reverence as our Constitution—its frailties at birth forgotten because of its vigor in maturity.

In Wilson's day Congress refused to risk our national sovereignty to international decision. The treaty shattered like glass when it collided with our caution. We have learned from the present war that the ostrich was vulnerably exposed despite the care with which it hid its head. We might have learned this lesson from our own Revolutionary founders. After the unsuccessful Articles of Confederation, they were willing to risk sovereign rights in the interest of peace. For example, the United States Supreme Court was the first international court of justice in the history of the world. It was the first court to which thirteen sovereign States subjected themselves to absolute decision.

To recognize the audacity of this innovation, one must mentally transplant himself to the year 1787. Furious patriotic debates raged in New York as to whether the sovereign State of New York could possibly surrender its independence to the whim of judicial decision made by judges of other rival States. George

Mason, the delegate who framed the Bill of Rights for the Virginia Constitution, refused to sign the United States Constitution partly on the ground that the Supreme Court was "so constructed and extended as to absorb and destroy the judiciaries of the several States; thereby * * * enabling the rich to oppress and ruin the poor."

We know now how the nation and the peace among the thirteen States were strengthened rather than weakened by this unprecedented pooling of sovereign rights.

In this respect we are not asked at San Francisco to pioneer in a completely untried realm. Dumbarton Oaks proposals set up an International Court. But there has been a Permanent Court of International Justice since 1921. It has functioned brilliantly despite feeble enforcement powers. It is a miracle that, left alone and undernourished, it did not wither and die. The peoples of the world ought to be made familiar with its achievements. For here is an object lesson of how international loyalties can be restrained in the interest of justice.

The judges of this court have been chosen in the following wise manner: Each member nation named four nominees, only two of whom could be nationals of the nominating state. Then the Assembly and Council of the League of Nations, acting separately, elected the judges by a majority rule. Since each nation was required to nominate two judges who were nationals of another nation, national partisanship was reduced to a minimum. This device has all the ingenuity which is attributed to the Greek generals who, after their victory over the Persians at Salamis, voted to select the best among them. Each general voted for himself, but each chose Themistocles as the second best. It was Themistocles who was properly chosen the winner.

It is encouraging that the Dumbarton Oaks proposal suggests the adoption of the Statute of the Permanent Court of International Justice or that it be used as a basis for a new statute.

Most of us are inclined to overstress the importance of the written provisions of the Dumbarton Oaks proposals and to underestimate the value of international consultation which it necessitates and for which it provides the forum. Governments are like clocks, they go from the motion that men give them. At San Francisco we have a new opportunity to establish a continuous motion devoted to balancing the peace.

San Francisco cannot heal the world. There will be a series of crises in the coming years. What else can one expect after the cataclysm we have passed through? But the test of international peace is not the absence of conflicts but how they are resolved.

In our Western pioneering days we passed through the transition from the "pistol is my law" era to the acceptance of judicial authority. It is not impossible or too late to make the same progress in international affairs. We have failed often in the past to preserve peace, but discouragement to try again would be the only lasting defeat. When Thomas Edison was asked whether he was making progress in his inventive search for a new battery, he replied, "Certainly, I have found 1,000 things that don't work." If we would pour into our efforts for peace the enormous strength and brilliant planning and resourcefulness which we devote to war, who can say that our triumph in peace would be less than in war?

If our Founding Fathers could attend at San Francisco, it is clear from their words when faced with similar problems regarding thirteen sovereign States, they would urge us to accept the Dumbarton Oaks proposals. They would tell us that these are the bricks and mortar of our continued unity, of our structure for peace. They would warn us not to tear down the building because we don't like the paint job here or there. They would plead with us to move into the building immediately, for if it is not occupied it will crack and fall apart. A home is made by living in it. There will be generations of time to improve it and make it a beautiful house of peace.

On the historic day when the delegates at the convention signed the United States Constitution, Benjamin Franklin looked toward the President's chair at the back of which a rising sun happened to be painted. He said: "I have often, in the course of the session, and the vicissitudes of my hopes and fears as to its issue, looked at [the sun] behind the President without being able to tell whether it was rising or setting; but now at length I have the happiness to know that it is a rising and not a setting sun."

The whole world hopes that when the San Francisco Conference has ended, the sun above the Golden Gate will be the rising sun of future peace.

Shield of Our Liberty: The Bill of Rights

by James Truslow Adams

IN A TIME when personal liberties are being trampled under foot and when personal vengeance is not only condoned but encouraged by totalitarian leaders, the great democracies must look again and with new concern to their Bills of Rights. In such documents lives the sum of man's victories over the forces of barbarism and oppression, and in their preservation lies the hope of man as a free individual.

The Bills of Rights have been abandoned in the totalitarian countries. In Great Britain and in France there has been complaint against unofficial censorships. In our own America we have seen free speech and free assembly challenged and upheld by the courts. Seeing these things, we cannot fail to realize that our own Bill of Rights, under the protection of the courts, is the sole guarantee of the liberties of the individual. It may be well if we examine more closely that guarantee.

What is the Bill of Rights? In America it is the body of principles laid down in the first ten amendments to the Constitution. Those principles embody what were then considered, and still are, the fundamental rights of free men.

From the *New York Times Magazine,* November 20, 1938, copyright © 1938, 1966 by The New York Times Company.

The first article specifically sets forth the four fundamental freedoms: "Congress," it reads, "shall make no law respecting an establishment of religion or prohibiting the free exercise thereof; or abridging the freedom of speech or of the press; or the right of the people peaceably to assemble and to petition the government for a redress of grievances."

Thence the document goes on to list and to specify personal rights. "The right of the people to keep and bear arms shall not be infringed. * * * No soldier shall, in time of peace, be quartered in any house without the consent of the owner, nor in war time but in a maner to be prescribed by law. * * * The right of the people to be secure in their persons, houses, papers and effects, against unreasonable searches and seizures, shall not be violated."

The right of free men to trial and justice is specified: "No person shall be held to answer for a capital or other infamous crime unless on a presentment or indictment of a grand jury. * * * Nor be deprived of life, liberty or property without due process of the law; nor shall private property be taken for public use without just compensation. * * * The accused shall enjoy the right to a speedy and public trial by an impartial jury. * * * No fact tried by a jury shall be otherwise reexamined in any court of the United States than according to the rules of common law. * * * Excessive bail shall not be required, nor excessive fines imposed, nor cruel and unusual punishments inflicted."

How vital do those articles appear when read again against the background of today's events in Europe! Not one or two, but all of those guarantees set down by our forefathers have been abridged in the totalitarian countries; not only abridged, but held up to scorn as the weakness of the democracies.

And the last two articles of our Bill of Rights take care to specify that in so enumerating certain rights there is no denial or disparagement of others retained by the people, and to make it clear that powers not specifically delegated to the national government are reserved to the States and to the people.

These were all rights for which our ancestors had fought against Great Britain. The denial of many of them is listed in the long indictment of George III which forms part of the Declaration of Independence; for example, when the complaints are made that he "transported us beyond the seas to be tried," that he deprived us "of the benefits of trial by jury," that he quartered "large bodies of armed troops among us," and so on.

They were not, therefore, matters of theory. The colonists had seen their leaders threatened with deportation and trial by hostile courts 3,000 miles away. They had seen their houses broken into and their papers ransacked by royal officials. They had seen charters of government taken from them; one of their most thriving ports was closed because of the unlawful acts of a handful of citizens; troops had been quartered among them. To prevent a recurrence of these things they had risked their lives and their fortunes.

The Bill of Rights did not go into force until 1791, more than two years after the new nation started its life under the new form of government. But the fact that such a Bill of Rights was not included in the original Constitution does not mean the framers did not believe that certain fundamental guarantees were essential to the maintenance of liberty. Before the Federal Constitution was drawn up many of the individual States had already adopted such Bills of Rights and the founding fathers believed that guarantees of liberty were sufficiently embodied in the State Constitutions. They also held that, since the Federal Government was to be one of limited powers only, it could not infringe on the rights guaranteed by the individual States. Indeed, Hamilton wrote in The Federalist that a Federal Bill of Rights might even be dangerous, because to declare that the Federal Government could not exercise certain powers which it did not possess might give it a pretext to claim them.

There was much logic in the arguments of Hamilton and others who opposed the inclusion of a Bill of Rights, but the people saw more clearly. They sensed that the Federal Government might in time come to have much power, and they knew from history and human nature that those in possession of power always wish to extend, if not to abuse it. Moreover, there was the clause in the Constitution which gave Congress the right to "make all laws which shall be proper and necessary" for the execution of the powers specifically granted to it. This clause might be construed to increase those powers enormously. The people had fought through an eight years' war to safeguard their liberties, and they were taking no chances in trusting even their own elective government.

Their judgment has been proved all too good; there have been many occasions when the personal freedom we cherish might have been destroyed without such a bill of guarantees and the Supreme Court to preserve them to us. Before citing illustrative instances we may note that although it is often erroneously said that the Constitution was enacted for the benefit of the conservative and propertied classes, the ten amendments constituting the Bill of Rights, which is the very heart and soul of the whole instrument, came straight from the insistent demand of the so-called "common," and to a large extent the radical, people—the farmers, town artisans and others as well as leaders of democracy like Jefferson and Madison.

So strongly, indeed, did the people feel about the fundamental guarantees against encroachments on their rights that the Constitution could not possibly have been adopted if the people of some of the more important States, such as Massachusetts and Virginia, had not been assured that as soon as it was adopted appropriate amendments would be recommended by Congress in the way provided under the instrument itself. There was no promise of specific amendments or draft of their wording, but it was thoroughly understood how the fundamental guarantees would be provided.

In accordance with the understanding James Madison, who had been elected to the first House of Representatives, arose in that body on June 8, 1789, less than two months after Washington took his oath of office as President, and, in a long speech, proposed that the Constitution be amended so as to remove the chief objections to it. Madison's proposed additions to the Constitution were referred to a select committee which reported back to the House a list of seventeen amendments. Twelve of these met with the approval of Congress and were sent to the State Legislatures for ratification on Sept. 25, 1789. The first two of the twelve had to do with the reapportionment of Congressional districts and the compensation of members of Congress. They were rejected by the States and amendments three to twelve inclusive were ratified as amendments one to ten, constituting our Bill of Rights, and became effective on Dec. 15, 1791. Since the rejected amendments did not involve fundamental rights, no guarantees of liberty were lost when they were voted down. But the first ten amendments have been a bulwark of freedom in this country from 1791 down to the present day.

Personal liberty in the past has been threatened by both the executive and legislative branches. In general the threats from the former have come in time of war, notably under Lincoln in the Civil War and under Wilson in the World War and following it. In both cases Congress to a large extent concurred. In 1919-20 freedom of speech and press, as well as other personal liberties, almost disappeared for the time being, the courts alone upholding them.

As early, however, as 1798 in the case of the Alien and Sedition Acts, particularly the latter, which allowed the Federalist party in power conveniently to jail or heavily fine annoying editors of the Republican party, the Bill of Rights had its first test and showed its worth. Congress has tried since to authorize illegal seizure of private papers (1886), the trial of a man the second time on the same charge (1870), the imprisonment of people at hard labor without any indictment by a grand jury (1890), the trial of a criminal without his being confronted by the witnesses against him (1899), and so on. Each time it has been blocked by the Supreme Court upholding, in the years named, the Bill of Rights.

We are so used to the exercise of these rights, and to being protected in them, that many of those who benefit from them overlook what such guarantees mean. Not only do they save us from oppression by the government, they also save minorities from being oppressed by laws drawn and passed by majorities. The Bill of Rights protects not merely property but the freedom of all to criticize government, to express themselves, and to start what movements for change they may wish. All new movements start with minorities, and if these amendments did not exist, or if Congress or the Executive could override the fundamental law or the courts, no citizens would suffer more than those "liberals" and radicals who so often denounce the Constitution. Written into the Constitution by the ordinary man those ten amendments remain today even more valuable to him than to any one else.

It is impossible to overrate the part which the Bill of Rights has played in building up the American tradition, the American dream and the American nation. America is not perfect, and like any other aggregation of human beings on a large scale our civilization is full of faults, abuses and maladjustments. None the less the various guarantees in the bill have given to the ordinary man and woman a sense of security in their property and homes, a sense of freedom to be and to express themselves in every way, which are to be found and experienced nowhere else in the world, past or present.

It has often been said that it is not our Constitution, but the abounding riches of the continent—which we have exploited carelessly and too rapidly—that built up our wealth, power and population. To some extent this is true, but without the guarantees of the Bill of Rights, protected by the courts, our own native citizens and the millions who have come to us from lands less free would not have had the incentive to build themselves up or that sense of safety and of liberty which has made the American different from the man or woman of all other nationalities, and which has acted so powerfully to develop the essential traits of our American character and civilization. America has been built not by free land, but by free men. That large sense of freedom which we have accepted as naturally as the air we breathe has come from the wise foresight of the ordinary Americans of 150 years ago who insisted that there should be no nation or Constitution at all unless guarantees of freedom from the tyrannies they had previously endured were deposited in the very cornerstones of both.

The rest of our Constitution and our whole theory of government, with its separation of powers and other essential elements, are of vast importance to us. It should be studied as it exists at present, not as it was before our last great constitutional crisis of the Civil War period. But the part which forms the Bill of Rights should be specially read and pondered by every one. As each clause is studied the reader should ask himself what might happen to him on some occasion if he no longer had such rights or such protection against an agent or department of government —instead of taking it for granted that he always must and will have that protection.

We are at present confronted by the storms of a new political philosophy, sweeping over nation after nation which we have hitherto considered as highly cultured and civilized, but in which personal rights and liberties now have largely ceased to exist. Think what has happened in Austria, in Czechoslovakia, and what now is happening in Germany. Point by point, one can go through our own Bill of Rights and see how each specific guarantee, once regarded as the right of man even there, has been swept away. There is no right of person or property. There is no right of trial. Cruel and unusual punishments have become commonplace, at the whim of a dictatorial agent. And the four fundamental freedoms were banished so completely and so early in the game that they are but a vague memory in the hearts of men and women in the concentration camps. Now, even the concentration camps pale into the background of a terror officially inspired against a whole section of the people whose only crime is in being a minority.

If there were ever a time in history when we should read again our guarantees and think of what they mean, surely it is now. Our freedom is unique, yet we take it for granted. Our courts still function, and they uphold the laws of our elected legislatures. We worship as we please. Our homes are safe from invasion by a

Gestapo or its equivalent. Our property cannot be confiscated. Our States maintain their powers, and our municipalities and towns and villages.

We are free to criticize, to assemble and debate the issues. Our vote is free and secret. Our press may speak its mind and print the news. Our minorities may organize and have their say and become majorities if that is the will of sufficient voters.

We are a free people because freedom has been the American ideal from the first days of the republic, an ideal embodied in the opening words of the Declaration of Independence and firmly planted in the Constitution. But freedom does not stand alone and of itself; it has taken centuries of time and oceans of blood to achieve and secure those elemental freedoms embodied in our Bill of Rights, and should they be lost the whole long and agonizing path might have to be trod once more before happier generations would know again such liberty of person and such freedom of spirit.

Freedom stands only so long as free men make it stand against the winds of intolerance and abuse. Our Bill of Rights shall stand, likewise, only so long as we realize and value the unique and fundamental freedoms of which it is the bulwark. Only so long as we are vigilant.

First Congress Was Not Unlike the 76th

by Seelye Jones

WHEN CONGRESS paused yesterday to commemorate the 150th anniversary of the First Congress of the United States of America, which met in New York on March 4, 1789, there was opportunity to observe how history repeats itself. The First Congress was confronted by almost all of the problems of the Seventy-sixth.

Probably the most notable difference between the situation of the First Congress and that of the present lies in the absence, at the earlier one, of a sense of the critical condition of the country, the lack of public pressure for a quick solution of all questions, and the want of any precedents. The statesmen of 150 years ago assembling to launch the new government under the untried Constitution, "met in an emergency," "faced a crisis," "stood at a crossroads," were "confronted with terrific problems," found the country "poised on the edge of a precipice"—and were so little excited about it that most of them arrived from one to six weeks late.

Although it was slow in getting started, the First Congress was to have plenty of excitement before it closed. It was to be confronted with the questions of taxes, tariff, war, a threat of

From the *New York Times Magazine,* March 5, 1939, copyright © 1939, 1967 by The New York Times Company.

secession, quarrels with the President about appointments, speculation, a national debt, a budget, States' rights, armaments, a merchant marine and banks.

That the new Congress solved some of these problems, under
the conditions surrounding its beginners, was no small achievement. That it did something about all of them, and many more,
and that what it did worked out reasonably well, is not short of
remarkable. It is true that the revenue act of its final session,
placing a tax on distilled spirits, gave rise to the Whisky Rebellion
in Western Pennsylvania and almost disrupted the new United
States; true that its debates and resolutions concerning our
relations with England and France were of a kind which in later
years would surely have produced a war with one or the other
of those countries. But, operating against a foreign war, communications were slow, the importance of this nation was not fully
established, and the English Crown, at least, had become accustomed to the acid tongues of the republicans overseas.

From the vantage of today the beginnings of the First Congress
appear frivolous. The Constitution had been formulated in 1787,
ratified successively by eleven States up to midsummer of 1788,
and the election of a President and a Congress had been carried
on in somewhat desultory fashion in the Autumn of that year.
North Carolina and Rhode Island had not ratified, and remained
separate States. New York had not yet elected Senators and
Representatives.

On the day set for the new government to take office eight
Senators were in the city and thirteen members of the House.
Until half the Senators and Representatives should appear it was
impossible to canvass the election returns and advise George
Washington that he was President of the United States, and John
Adams that he was Vice President. Not until April 6 did the
Senate have a quorum, at which time it elected John Langdon of
New Hampshire its temporary president, and met with the House
to canvass the electoral votes.

Messengers were sent off to Virginia and Massachusetts to
advise the President and Vice President of the result. Adams rode

into town on April 21 and took over the presiding office of the Senate. Washington proceeded slowly by coach from Mount Vernon, reached New York on the 23rd, and on April 30 was sworn in at Federal Hall. The United States, which had been virtually without a government since the Continental Congress had ceased to muster a quorum in the previous Autumn, was at last a going concern.

The city, which received the Federal statesmen, had enjoyed such prestige as may have come from the later sittings of the Continental Congress. Several Ministers from foreign countries were resident here. There had been time for the reconstruction of the old City Hall, at Wall and Broad Streets, where the Sub-treasury now stands, into Federal Hall, and Major L'Enfant's handsome plan had made of it a building almost wholly new. The French engineer had consulted the Constitution, providing meeting halls for both houses, committee rooms and offices, and furniture of style and comfort. There was a special double chair in the Senate Chamber, which he conceived might fit the President and Vice President jointly on occasion. The Osgood House, prepared for General Washington, was a mansion of no mean proportions.

Otherwise the city had many aspects of a boom town. Its 30,000 people were crowding its narrow confines on the lower tip of Manhattan Island. It had two banks, considerable shipping and daily coach and mail service to Boston and Philadelphia. A few oil lamps lighted the streets at night, and there was a theatre to which the new President went to see "The School for Scandal."

The members of the new Congress were not ignorant of what lay before them, for seventeen of the Senators and thirty-four of the Representatives had served at one time or another in the Continental Congress. Present were many of the notables of the Revolutionary period, and some who would acquire further fame in years ahead. Oliver Ellsworth of Connecticut, who might be termed the leader of the Federalists in the Senate, was to become Chief Justice; Richard Henry Lee of Virginia, the leader of the opposition, had been a signer of the Declaration and a President of the Continental Congress, in which he offered the resolution for independence. Senator James Monroe of Virginia was to become President of the United States. There were also Robert Morris of Pennsylvania, Charles Carroll of Carrollton and Ralph Izard of South Carolina.

Equally brilliant were the leaders in the lower house, where sat James Madison of Virginia. Jonathan Trumbull of Connecticut at 39 had yet ahead of him seven terms as Governor, one as Speaker of the House, one as Senator and behind him service as aide de camp to Washington. John Sevier of North Carolina had been Governor of the unrecognized State of Franklin for three years, and would live to govern Tennessee and serve here in the Twelfth, Thirteenth and Fourteenth Congresses. Roger Sherman of Connecticut had signed, in turn, the declaration of 1774, the Declaration of Independence, the Articles of Confederation and the Constitution. No other name is on all of them. Elbridge Gerry, who would become Vice President in 1812, was an anti-Federalist from Masaschusetts. He would have a grandson in the House and a great-grandson in the Senate, where Peter Goelet Gerry of Rhode Island sits today.

Meetings prior to Washington's inauguration had been devoted chiefly to discussions of titles and procedure. How should the President be addressed? How should the two houses communicate with one another? Should a member or a clerk carry the messages? Should he be received at the door, or at the bar of the House, with the members seated, or standing? What form of address would be applicable to the Vice President, to the Speaker of the House?

To such details John Adams, experienced at the English court, where he had represented the Colonies, gave powerful attention. He spoke freely and fully to the Senate, advising dignity, form, ceremony. When Washington finally appeared before the Congress, the worthy Vice President was practically in a dither. Where should he stand with reference to the President, and when should he sit? Should he be covered or uncovered? What was the proper form of address? The answer of Congress to Washington's Inaugural Address referred to "His Most Gracious Speech." A communication from Poland referred to the President as "His Elective Majesty." "Elective Highness" was suggested as his title. Adams spoke for an hour against the indignity of calling him merely "Mister President."

Deep in such a quandary, the Congress nevertheless realized that a nation must have a revenue, and the first bill, for a tonnage tax on shipping and a tariff on imports, was proposed. With it came the natural host of local claims, trades, log-rollings, which have accompanied tariff legislation for the succeeding century and a half. New England united against 6 cents a gallon on molasses. The tariff was cut to 4. Pennsylvania wanted its sugar refineries protected. The old revolutionists wanted the tonnage tax higher on British than on French shipping. It was over the tariff bill that Pierce Butler, a Senator from South Carolina, uttered the threat of secession by his State—a threat which would be renewed more than once before it was carried out in 1860 over another and even more bitter set of issues.

Before the revenue bill had passed on July 1, the Congress was working on a bill to establish a Federal judiciary, was wrestling with the proper language for the oath of office of all Federal officials, and the Senate was asserting its prerogatives respecting Presidential appointments and considering just how it would "advise and consent" regarding the nomination of Mr. Short to succeed Mr. Jefferson as Ambassador to France.

Here was the start of the eternal question of patronage. President Washington merely sent in his nominations. Was this asking the Senate for advice? Or merely for consent? The Executive Departments Bill was pending. Would the President appoint these executives merely with "consent"? And did the Senate have power of removal, as well as of approval? That question went to a tie vote, 10 to 10, on July 16. Vice President Adams voted to retain the clause giving the removal power solely to the President. William Maclay, a Senator from Pennsylvania, who kept the most complete diary of the First Congress, noted this as a victory for the "Court Party" and accused James Madison, an authority on the

Constitution, of having favored Presidential power of removal because he wished to flatter Washington.

On August 22 the Senate had its first opoprtunity to consent to a treaty with a foreign power. President Washington came in person to present the proposal for a treaty with certain hostile Indians. The proposals were entirely new to the Senators, but Vice President Adams thought they ought to be adopted at once, without debate.

Maclay had the temerity to arise and question the President of the United States, who allowed General Knox, the potential Secretary of War, to answer. The whole matter was postponed until the Senate could learn more about it. That evening General Washington sent Maclay an invitation to dinner. The intrepid Pennsylvanian recorded in his journal that he would accept, but that the President need not think he could "get around me" by social favors.

This Pennsylvanian was a member of the "left"; he favored just as little authority in the new central government as possible under a strict interpretation of the Constitution. He saw no occasion to have a Secretary of War, asserting that such an official would at once want a standing army, and given an army would certainly start a war. Maclay thought the State militias were adequate. He opposed the naming of Ambassadors to countries in Europe, saying that we had no arguments with lands over the sea and needed no agent there. He respected Washington as "the greatest man in the world," but suspected that the President was being used by Hamilton and the bankers and merchants and "speculators" of New York.

The first session of the First Congress ended on September 29, 1789, and the second session assembled in New York on January 4, 1790. Twelve of the States were represented, Rhode Island alone holding aloof from the Union. (She was to ratify late in May of that year.) By this time the courts were functioning, five executive departments were in operation and tariff and tonnage taxes were supporting the Union.

Two outstanding problems were to worry the second and third

sessions: one, the location of the permanent capital, the other the funding of the war debts of the Continental Congress and of the several States. Over these issues the political parties which were to become the Federalists and the Republicans began to shape, the North and South to divide, the trading and negotiating and jockeying for votes to increase.

Alexander Hamilton had rapidly become the most industrious and the most powerful man in the government and leader of the Federalists, the party of strong central government. He had in general the backing of the New Englanders, the New Yorkers and, on the funding and assumption issue, of the South Carolinians, for South Carolina and Massachusetts had the heaviest claims for outlays during the late war. This group of States mustered 28 of the 65 votes in the House.

The politics of the second session and some of the third session may be said to have hinged around the efforts of the Hamiltonians to win over either Pennsylvania, with 8 votes, or Virginia, with 10. The prize offered in turn to these delegations was the location of the capital city. In the early stages of the second session Pennsylvania seemed in a fair way to get the "permanent residence" of the government. Most of its Representatives, however, and one of its Senators, Maclay, were unwilling to give support to the funding and assumption bills; and the delegation was divided as to the site within the State at which the "permanent residence" should stand.

The Federalists, playing for time, kept New York in line by holding out hopes of her retaining the "temporary residence" for five or ten years; they listened to Maryland's claim for Baltimore and Virginia's suggestion of a site on the Potomac. Meanwhile there was great speculation in the State certificates of debt which would be validated at 100 cents on the dollar if the assumption passed. The outcome was a triumph for the Federalists on the funding and assumption bills and a compromise by which Philadelphia got the temporary residence for ten years. The Potomac, of course, got the capital.

Maclay, who gives us the detailed story of the Congress in

the year 1790, fought and fumed against the Hamiltonians but always lost. He set forth pretty frankly in his diary the opinion that the Hamiltonians were "lacking in candor" and once he offered to his journal a doubt that any honest man lived east of the Hudson River. New York City he despised.

At the end of his two years in Congress this intransigent Senator who was not re-elected visualized the downfall of State authority, with all men of talent seeking the high salaries and perquisites of Federal positions. Such offices were being created and multiplied, he wrote, in the diplomatic, judiciary and military establishments.

"This," he wrote, "is called giving the President a respectable patronage—a term, I confess, new to me in the present sense of it, which I take to mean neither more nor less than the President should always have a number of lucrative places in his gift to reward those members of Congress who may promote his views or support his measures; more especially if by such conduct they should forfeit the esteem of their constituents."

Thus the lame duck had early raised his ugly head.

The papers of Madison and others give a better picture of the constructive job which was accomplished in putting a new government into operation. The finances were established on a solid basis and the United States Bank was founded. A postal system was developed. A Federal judiciary was set up. Whether the establishment of the Union brought prosperity, or prosperity helped the establishment of the Union, the times improved, trade flourished, peace was maintained, Western development was pushed, Kentucky and Vermont were added to the list of States, whiskey was taxed, a navy was proposed to battle the Algerian pirates, an army to cope with the hostile tribes to the west and south. Before the First Congress had adjourned a survey line had bounded the ten-mile square on which the capital city would be built.

The third and final session was held at Philadelphia from December 6, 1790, to March 3, 1791. On the last day there was a terrific rush of legislation. The clerks were fairly swamped, the President's secretaries came and went, messengers passed back and forth from House to Senate, and yet all could not be done on time. A great banquet had been set for the afternoon, and the Congress had to reassemble for its first night session.

The members gathered in a jovial mood, rushed through a final mass of bills, including some salary increases, appropriation measures, a law to establish a mint, a pension bill, a lighthouse bill. It was a tiring occasion for the clerks, who must write all matters in longhand; a final futility for Senator Maclay, objecting and protesting to his last hour in Congress; a gala moment for many of the members, who had dined and drunk well at the banquet. They did not have to set the clock back. Before midnight the First Congress of the United States had made its final mark in history.

Part 3

THE REVOLUTION AS A CONTINUING PROCESS

IF HISTORY OFFERS any lesson it is the uniqueness of every event. The American Revolution stands by itself as a monument to the vitality and inventiveness of a particular age. Each generation has appealed to it for inspiration and guidance, and each has found within it contradictory themes. To some it has been a radical break with the past; to others it has been a most conservative development.

Dumas Malone has noted the parallels between the American and French Revolutions, but he finds the early appearance of differences far more significant. Americans had nothing to destroy; Frenchmen had nothing to preserve. Malone also notes that revolutions traditionally move from right to left in the political spectrum, a truism which aptly describes the French movement—but not the American. This departure of the American Revolution from classic patterns emphasizes its unique qualities.

Henry Steele Commager talks about the Revolutionary era's creativity. He distinguishes between the Revolution, which he suggests began about 1760 and reached a peak in 1787, and the War for Independence. As a broader movement, the Revolution has much greater significance for Commager. He hints that it is a continuing process with no end in sight. Its creativity, he adds, is suggested by its concern with the creation of a new empire rather than the destruction of an old one.

Whether or not the Revolution is a continuing process, Americans certainly continue to argue its premises. Our national tranquility has often been disturbed by arguments over the key issue which brought on the upheaval of 1776—the relationship between the states and the central government. The revolution by no means settled this dispute. It was raised anew in 1798–99 when Madison and Jefferson attacked the Alien and Sedition Acts; Calhoun revived it in his challenge to Jackson over the South Carolina Nullification Controversy; it formed a critical issue leading to the Civil War; it became the focus of controversy when New Deal reform legislation intruded federal authority into traditional state jurisdictions; and the South used it as a defense against recent federal civil rights legislation.

In defending or attacking solutions to contemporary problems, Americans have often relied upon the philosophy of the Founding Fathers. Indeed, they frequently cloak modern social or economic issues with philosophical concepts wrenched bodily from the words of the Revolutionary era. There is a ludicrous quality to arguments which use the language of Jefferson and Hamilton, especially since neither man ever envisaged the problems faced by modern society. Yet, by providing Americans with a common standard and a rhetoric to use in measuring men, issues, and events, the Founding Fathers have served us well. While people argue over the meaning and implications of sacred phrases from the past, there is less likelihood of their taking to the barricades.

One illustration of how this debate has punctuated our history is provided by the essays of James Truslow Adams and Henry Steele Commager, written in the heat of controversy over New

Deal regulatory legislation. Adams emphasized the Founding Fathers' suspicions of power, whether lodged in a central government, state government, or in the people. The Constitutional convention, he asserts, intended an equilibrium of power in order to preserve individual liberty. Thus the Fathers wanted a controlled government, not a strong one. Commager, on the contrary, argues that the federal system has evolved naturally from the framework of 1787, and he views the Constitution as a realistic document rather than a theoretical one. Thus the original division of power was based on experience instead of ideology. To Commager, federalism is an ever-changing relationship between the people and the two levels of authority—state and federal—that they created. Its essential ingredient, therefore, is its fluidity and adaptability.

Such debates as this, extending back through the whole fabric of our history, have kept alive the American Revolution's heritage. As long as Americans find it profitable to explore the Founding Fathers' words and deeds, they will expand and enrich the Revolution's meaning. Americans in the British Empire in 1776 were unable to find useful meanings in their British past. Should the American past become as rigid for us as the British past did for Americans in 1776, the nation may once again be ready to mount the barricades.

Paradox of the American Revolution

by Dumas Malone

GEORGE WASHINGTON rose to fame as the military leader of a revolutionary cause, and he was regarded both at home and abroad as the symbol and embodiment of that cause. Yet the main impression he made on his contemporaries and left to history was not that of a radical or revolutionary, as we commonly use those terms today. Of him, a foreign visitor said that he was renowned throughout the world for his wisdom and moderation, and Thomas Jefferson, who had abundant opportunity to observe him, said that the most notable feature of his character was prudence.

His career, therefore, seems paradoxical. In considering it we are impelled to ask just what sort of revolution this was that he symbolized and personified. Did it proceed from moderation to excess and terror, as the revolutions in France and Russia did? Was it followed by reaction and counter-revolution? Or was it in a pattern of its own, and was Washington himself a revolutionary leader without historic counterpart?

One obvious difference between it and the later world-shaking revolutions in France and Russia is that ours was a movement

From the *New York Times Magazine,* February 21, 1960, copyright © 1960 by The New York Times Company.

for national independence. In this respect, it can be more appropriately compared with later revolts of colonies against imperialism, but it bears only superficial resemblance to twentieth-century movements in Asia and Africa against European rule. Except for the slaves, our people were European, and all except a very small minority recognized Britain as their mother country. Our patriot forefathers fought a civil war within an empire bound together by common institutions and a common language. There was no need to repudiate these and start from scratch. For this reason, the transition from what they called "colonial subservience" to national independence was relatively easy, and the process of creating national institutions was more evolutionary than revolutionary.

The British colonists in North America had enjoyed for decades a degree of personal freedom probably unequaled in the world. The "tyranny" that was described in the Declaration of Independence was associated with the reign of George III, when, as was often asserted, "arbitrary domination" began. It was relative to the liberty that had existed previously. For this reason, in later years, John Jay objected to the expression, "our glorious *emancipation* from Britain," as used in a sermon on the death of Washington.

He viewed these matters as a conservative, but it is impossible to deny his contention that the struggle with the mother country began as an effort to *restore* old rights, liberties and privileges. Our patriot forefathers were well versed in local self-government, and, by and large, their local political institutions were probably more democratic than any other in the world at that time.

The American rebels were so much better prepared for national independence and self-government than the colonies of European powers which afterward revolted, as in Latin America, that no close parallel can be drawn. Yet it is a fact of history that our country has provided a shining example to peoples seeking to throw off foreign rule. It is equally true that our patriots gave to the world in the Declaration of Independence a charter of human rights which has had a continuing influence on those struggling against oppression everywhere. Its voice is that of human aspiration, not merely that of emerging nationality, and as a challenge to all existing tyranny in the name of universal human rights it was clearly revolutionary.

Herein lies the kinship of the American Revolution with revolts elsewhere against tyrannies far greater than our forefathers suffered—with revolts leading to cataclysms, as in France and Russia, the like of which Americans never had to face. There were many reasons why our historic experience was relatively so fortunate, but the matter can perhaps be summed up by saying that, because of their traditions, training, leadership and physical situation, Americans were able to realize their aspirations progressively with only slight recourse to force, once they assumed full control of their affairs. Unlike the revolutionaries in France, they were able to proceed by the regular processes of deliberation and legislation. Circumstances permitted them to be moderate, and if not wholly wise they were wiser than most.

Students of the French Revolution who have taken a world view—such as Crane Brinton and Robert R. Palmer—find numerous parallels between the early stages of that revolution and the American. George Washington shared the opinion of the latter that they "proceeded from the same principles." On receiving from his friend Lafayette the key to the Bastille, he described this as "the token of victory gained by liberty over despotism."

Partisans of the French uprising against an unjust and despotic system linked it with the earlier American revolt and invoked the name of Washington. Thomas Paine dedicated the first part of his famous pamphlet, "The Rights of Man," to the first President of the United States. "I present you a small treatise in defense of those principles of freedom which your exemplary virtue hath so eminently contributed to establish," he said. And he prayed that Washington might "enjoy the happiness of seeing the New World regenerate the Old."

Even at this stage, when France still had a king, the great American who was so noted for his prudence feared that things were going too fast in that country, but he did not yet doubt that they were going in the right direction.

Differences between the revolutions in the two worlds soon appeared, but in the early stages these were not ideological. As Benjamin Franklin's old friend, Madame d'Houdetot, wrote Jefferson, "The characteristic difference between your revolution and ours is that having nothing to destroy, you had nothing to injure." That was not quite true, for American patriots, besides destroying tea, applied tar and feathers upon occasion and confiscated a very considerable amount of Loyalist property. Still there was relatively little that the sovereign people needed or wanted to erase.

As Professor Brinton has said, the characteristic course of a revolution is from Right to Left, and the adoption of the Declaration of Independence marked the triumph of our "radicals." But Thomas Jefferson was no more a Robespierre and John Adams no more a Lenin than George Washington was a Castro. Compared to the Jacobins and Bolsheviks, our radicals were really moderates, believing in liberty under law and thoroughly accustomed to representative government. On their way to power they created extralegal agencies, such as Committees of Correspondence and committees to enforce the Continental Association, but they followed traditional political patterns when they could.

The patriots disowned the King and ousted the royal governors; nevertheless, in both the new states and the new confederation they adopted constitutions. That characteristic American institution, the constitutional convention, did not appear at once; but the idea of basic written law, to which even legislatures were subject, was present from the beginning, and the very existence of the state governments provided a constant check on the growth of power at the center.

It is hard to see how such a body as the famous Committee of Public Safety, through which the extremists ruled France, could ever have functioned in the American situation. It was our country's good fortune, also, that the patriots in Congress faced no such internal dangers as the Jacobins did in the conduct of the war. The Commander in Chief constituted no problem except to the impatient and the envious. From the time that he first buckled on his sword, Washington never failed to recognize the subordination of the military to the civil authority, nor neglected his manners toward the latter.

Often his situation and the future of his cause seemed desperate, and had not French aid been forthcoming more desperate measures might have been called for. He might have been supplanted by a less responsible and less humane commander, better suited to guerrilla warfare. But, as things turned out, he gained such a hold on the confidence of the country that replacement of him became unthinkable. He held things together by sheer force of character, and Congress managed to muddle through, without resort to the tyrannical rule of a little group of extremists.

Insofar as we had a Terror, it consisted largely of the proscription of the Loyalists and the confiscation of their property in the several states, and of various forms of pressure exerted by the patriots in their efforts to whip up enthusiasm and silence opposition.

There may have been much more of this sort of thing than we like to think, and no doubt we should be more aware of it if the loyalists had returned, as the émigrés did to France, and reminded posterity of their grievances. But it never extended to executions and massacres, and the patriots did not maintain themselves in power by exciting class warfare.

In France, after the Terror came Thermidor when Robespierre was overthrown and the rule of the extremists ended. Later came Napoleon, and at long last the restoration of the Bourbon monarchy. Thus the revolution was brought full cycle. In Russia it has not yet done that, and it may not in the foreseeable future, but there have been some signs of reaction even there.

What of the aftermath of Yorktown? Since there was no such crisis here as in France, and no comparable Terror, there was no such occasion for a Thermidor. There was grave danger of disintegration, but counter-revolution was not strongly threatened from within or without. The danger of a military *coup d'état,* like Napoleon's, was quickly proved nonexistent.

One threat, arising from the not unnatural discontent of unpaid soldiers at the very end of the war, took the form of a movement to make Washington king. Colonel Lewis Nicola broached the subject to the General in a letter and received a stern rebuke. No occurrence during the war, Washington said, had given him more "painful sensations" than the information that such ideas existed in the army.

At the same time he was deeply anxious that justice be done the army. As far as his powers and influence extended "in a constitutional way" he was determined to employ them to the utmost for his veterans. That patient General's remedy for the ills of the neglected soldiers was not to appeal to force but to represent their cause strongly and persistently to Congress. He never ceased to be a devoted republican and scrupulous constitutionalist.

Other signs of reaction, arising from discontent, were visible in the years immediately following the war, when the General was again a gentleman planter at Mount Vernon. In this relatively chaotic period the movement for a stronger central government and a more perfect Union got under way. This movement, which led to the framing and ratifying of the Constitution under which we still live, has been viewed by some as a sort of American Thermidor, just as the adoption of the Declaration of Independence has been viewed as the triumph of our "radicals."

Clearly it marked a swing to the Right, whether small or great, but the leaders of it, if not precisely the same men who signed the Declaration, were of similar status and fortune. The signers of the Declaration appear to have been richer, if anything. They were the same sort of men in a different situation. It is certainly a notable fact that George Washington, who had personified the revolutionary cause, presided over the Federal Convention in Philadelphia. He may be said to have presided over the whole movement, and without his blessing it could hardly have succeeded.

The framers of the Constitution, while strengthening the central government, undoubtedly tried to safeguard the institution of private property, to support public order and to reduce the danger of democratic excess. In the course of the ratification fight the supporters of the new instrument indulged in some high-handed actions, but the procedure as a whole warranted the praise given it by the author of the Declaration of Independence.

"The example of changing a constitution by assembling the wise men of the State, instead of assembling armies," Jefferson said, "will be worth as much to the world as the former examples we have given them." To his mind, the New World was still setting a pattern for the Old.

Furthermore, the framers of the Constitution wrote into our highest law the basic doctrine of the revolution in both worlds, the sovereignty of the people. This instrument was ratified by state conventions, specially chosen for this particular purpose and supposed to represent the popular will; and in its very first words it claimed that the people of the United States ordained it. The expression, "We the people," in the Preamble, left no room for doubt where the final authority and ultimate power really lay. The Constitution deflected the course of the Revolution somewhat, but it also implemented and established that Revolution. It left plenty of leeway for the development of a more popular government as well as a more perfect Union.

Reaction continued for a time after the institution of the new government with Washington as President. This reaction merged with revulsion against the excesses of the French Revolution, as these occurred and became known. Jefferson, who retained his ardor longer than his major colleagues, feared that if the counter-revolutionary cause, which was backed up by the armies of European kings from 1792 and 1793 onward, should triumph abroad, counter-revolution would be facilitated at home.

The nearest approach to counter-revolution in the United States was made toward the end of the century, when supposed foreign danger led to domestic repression. Partisans of Jefferson described this as a reign of terror, but the era of the Alien and Sedition Acts was marked by no bloodshed. Furthermore, he and Madison checked the reactionary political trend when they took over the government in 1801, after what he rather extravagantly termed the Revolution of 1800. It would be more correct to say that the continuance of the original American Revolution was then assured by the exercise of wholly constitutional means and with recourse to no force except the power of persuasion.

What course would Western history have taken if this Revolution had never happened?

If the quarrel with the mother country had been patched up without the loss of liberties previously enjoyed, and if these colonies had eventually evolved into a British dominion, conceivably the world might have seen a long-continued *Pax Britannica*. But our own country would scarcely have become an asylum for all peoples to the extent that it did and the development of democratic institutions would probably have been slowed down. It seems unlikely that the monarchies and aristocrats of Europe would have yielded much ground except under coercion, and Europe would have held America back.

Other interesting speculations come to mind, but it is sufficient to say here that the initial blame for the American revolt, and for the far more destructive uprising in France, must be laid on the ruling classes.

One of the most notable facts about the American Revolution is that its greatest leaders were themselves relatively privileged persons who, at the same time, recognized the primacy of human rights and sought to further these in the national interest and for the sake of a more just society. Also, the movement was notable for the continuity of its leadership, and without this it would hardly have been as moderate and as constructive as it turned out to be.

John Adams, while Vice President, predicted that successive groups of leaders would gain power in France, that each of these would destroy its predecessors, and that eventually there would be the rule of force. Subsequent events in that country demonstrated his prescience, and in our time the same thing could be said about Russia. But nothing of the sort had happened or did happen in America, except only for the ejection of the Loyalists. Some men, notably Adams and Jefferson, were leaders throughout the whole of the revolutionary generation, extending to the end of the century.

George Washington did not last quite that long, and toward the very end of his life he was caught up in reaction to some degree, but for a score of years at least he remained the central and symbolic figure, and he provided continuity when it was needed most. That was his supreme service.

In his classic description of Washington in his own old age, before Bonaparte had been overthrown, Jefferson said that "his was the singular destiny and merit of leading the armies of his country successfully through an arduous war for the establishment of its independence; of conducting its councils through the birth of a government, new in its forms and principles, until it had settled down into a quiet and orderly train; and of scrupulously obeying the laws through the whole of his career, civil and military, of which the history of the world furnishes no other example."

In later history parallels can be found to the revolution Washington led, especially in its first phases, but that movement still occupies a distinctive place in the human story and there is strong ground for the judgment that as a revolutionary leader Washington is still unique.

Our Beginnings:
A Lesson for Today

by Henry Steele Commager

THOUSANDS OF Americans now are reading Oliver Wiswell's nar-
rative of the American Revolution, as told by Kenneth Roberts,
and are learning for the first time that there was a Loyalist as well
as a Patriot side to this family quarrel of the Seventeen Seventies.
They are discovering, with a sense of surprise not a little curious,
that the war was not a sedate affair staged for the edification of
future professional patriots, but that it had—like all wars and
all revolutions—its seamy side; that the patriot fathers were not
figures on pedestals posing for posterity, but flesh-and-blood men
busy with fighting and politics, and that an accounting for the
whole episode reveals some items on the debit as well as on the
credit side.

In many quarters, indeed, there are indications of the emergence of an attitude faintly apologetic toward the whole affair—a
feeling that the Revolutionary Fathers were guilty of unseemly
conduct or, at least, of short-sightedness in surrendering the
solid advantages of the British connection for the uncertain consequences of popular government. Perhaps the time is not un-

From the *New York Times Magazine,* January 26, 1941, copyright © 1941,
1969 by The New York Times Company.

propitious for a reappraisal of the American Revolution and a determination of its more significant contributions.

What, after all, do we know about this period of our history? We can answer that question briefly by saying that we know more than we did, but less than we ought. The researches of scholars have brought to light many facts unknown to an earlier generation of students, while new points of view and perspective have suggested new meanings for old and familiar facts. The large framework of the Revolutionary period has been filled with countless details and, at the same time, these details have been woven into new patterns. Space does not permit any evaluation of the new facts, but we can suggest something of the new patterns.

First, then, what of the term itself? Here we encounter an initial difficulty—and a very old one. As early as 1787 Benjamin Rush was complaining that "there is nothing more common than to confound the terms of American Revolution with those of the late American war," and a century and a half later the confusion is still common. If we hope to understand what went on in this country in the last third of the eighteenth century, we must cut through this confusion. We must recognize the distinction between the American Revolution and the War for Independence.

The Revolution itself was a great creative movement that set in about 1760 and came to a close with the establishment of the Federal Government in 1789. The War for Independence was merely a part of this larger movement. It was, to be sure, an all-important part, for by breaking the bonds which tied the American Colonies to the mother country, it released those profound revolutionary forces which in the end created a new nation and a new democracy.

A realization of this will go far to correct many of the misinterpretations and misrepresentations of the Revolution—those advanced by the Oliver Wiswells as well as those cherished by the professional patriots. It will bring home to us the essential fact—too often ignored—that the Revolution was a constructive rather than a destructive period. It is not the disruption of one empire that is important; it is the creation of a new one. It is not the failure of British statesmanship to solve imperial problems that should command our attention; it is the success of Americans in finding solutions to those problems. It is not the dumping of tea or the burning of stamps or the rioting and tarring and feathering that we should remember, but the great fundamental institutions which were fashioned during these years of war and travail and which have done service for us from that day to the present.

What we have to understand, then, is a war which gave independence to the American people and a revolution out of which emerged a new society, a new economy, and new political institutions. For we must always keep in mind that—the felicitous phrasing of Carl Becker—the Revolution involved two things: home rule and the question who should rule at home. The first had to do with the problem of governmental organization; the second with the problem of democracy. Let us look briefly at these two aspects of the American Revolution.

The question of home rule was, of course, part of the larger question of imperial organization—a question not too dissimilar from that which has agitated our own generation with respect to world organization. England had developed, by the close of the Seven Years' War, a world empire, and she didn't know what to do with it.

Particularly difficult were the problems presented by the English colonies strung out along the Eastern seaboard of North America. For here had come to maturity an American people, restless under restraint, self-sufficient and self-conscious and self-assertive. Here had developed an American economy which did not readily accommodate itself to the larger economy of the empire or to the greed of English merchants, manufacturers, and land speculators. Here had evolved political institutions, stemming, to be sure, from the English but characteristically American.

Americans, over 2,000,000 strong and conscious of their strength, felt that politics and economy ought to be managed by them, and for their benefit. Englishmen, long accustomed to subordinate the interest of colonials to their own, insisted that Parliament knew best what should be done about American economy and government. There was no tyranny here, or no tyrannous purpose; there was inertia and blundering and greed, and the English did not have a monopoly on these unfortunate traits.

As we can see now, what was at issue was the organization of an empire. How could the American colonies be integrated into the larger empire in a manner that would strengthen the empire as a whole but not impair the interests or the welfare of the colonies? British statesmanship was unable to solve this problem, and the War for Independence is a monument to its failure.

The problem of organizing thirteen independent States into one nation, however, still remained. It was not solved by the Declaration of Independence, or by Yorktown, or by the Treaty of Paris of 1783. Could Americans work out a solution to this vexatious problem? Could they find a way to achieve national order and unity without sacrificing the liberties of individuals and the rights of States?

They could, and they did. The first attempt—the Articles of Confederation—was a failure. It was not as bad as some later critics described it, but it did fail to provide a firm basis for national unity. The second attempt was a success. That was the Federal Constitution, under which we are still living today. This Constitution did provide a way whereby national unity could be assured and the rights and liberties of individuals and of States preserved. It guaranteed home rule in all matters of local concern and secured national control over all matters of general concern. It solved the old problem of imperial organization by the new device of federalism. From the point of view of practical politics, that was the greatest contribution of the American Revolution, and its influence has not been limited to the United States but has been world-wide.

And along with federalism went another contribution that emerged from this period of struggle and disorder and experimentation. That was the creation of a new colonial system. Ever since the beginnings of the modern expansion of Europe, European nations had founded colonies and had regarded these colonies as existing for the benefit of the mother country. England was perhaps the most enlightened of the great colonizing powers, but in England, as elsewhere in the eighteenth-century world, colonies were something to be exploited.

Now when the United States achieved independence, it won, as one of the fruits of victory, the great expanse of territory westward from the Alleghenies to the Mississippi. Here was an American empire, an American colony. Here were lands to be settled, frontiers to be defended, resources to be exploited, governments to be administered. Should the new nation adopt the traditional policy of European nations toward colonial possessions? If not, what policy should be adopted?

The colonial policy that the new nation did adopt was the most enlightened of modern times. The statesmen of the Confederation took the revolutionary position that colonies did not exist for the benefit of the mother country but for the benefit of their inhabitants. As early as 1780, while the fight for independence was still going on, the legislators at Philadelphia promised that any lands ceded to the United States "shall be disposed of for the common benefit of the United States, and shall be settled and formed into distinct republican States, which shall become members of the Federal Union, and have the same rights of sovereignty, freedom, and independence as the other States."

This promise was faithfully kept. The Northwest Ordinance of 1787 provided for the speedy organization of national territory into States and the admission of these new States into the original Union on a basis of absolute equality. It established a new colonial policy and a new national policy, and on the basis of that policy the United States has expanded westward to the Pacific, growing from thirteen to forty-eight States, with so little friction that the average American is unaware that any policy has been involved or that the United States ever had a colonial problem.

Here, then, was what emerged out of the agitation of the

problem of home rule—a federal system and a new colonial policy. Both were original, both wonderfully constructive. What of the other basic question—who should rule at home?

This question, it will readily be seen, is none other than the question of democracy. And just as the Federal Constitution and the Northwest Ordinance present the principles of federalism and of colonial administration, so the Declaration of Independence presents the principles of democracy and equality. For the significance of the Declaration of Independence is not, paradoxically enough, in its announcement of independence; it is rather in its classic formulation of the philosophy of government to which Americans have since that time subscribed. For an understanding of the American Revolution—and indeed of all American history—the preamble to the Declaration is far more important than the body of the document.

What is the philosophy, what are the principles, of this memorable preamble? The opening lines of the Declaration are, of course, familiar to all Americans. They announce, as self-evident truths, certain fundamental principles: that all men are created equal, that they are endowed with unalienable rights, that among these rights are life, liberty, and the pursuit of happiness, that to preserve these rights is the purpose of government, that government is derived from the consent of the governed, and that if government is destructive of the rights of men it is the right and duty of men to alter or abolish it and to institute new governments. The history of the American Revolution is very largely the history of the actualization, the legalization, the institutionalization, of these principles.

To understand this we must keep in mind something of the social and economic situation in the American Colonies on the eve of the Revolution. We must keep in mind the fact that though the question of home rule in the empire made the headlines, the question of who was to rule at home was what interested the average man. The fact is that there was quite as much dissatisfaction with the way things were run in the Colonies as with the way things were run in Parliament.

We think of Patrick Henry denouncing the tyranny of George III, of Sam Adams organizing the Mohawks to spill tea in Boston Harbor, of Thomas Jefferson penning a Declaration which listed examples of royal despotism, of Benjamin Franklin cementing the French alliance. But Henry was the leader of the back-country dissenters, the flaming radical who fought the tidewater gentry; Adams was the master of the Boston town meeting, the agitator of leveling principles; Jefferson was the great democrat who planned to revolutionize government and society in the Old Dominion; Franklin was the spokesman of the back-country Germans and Scotch-Irish who inspired the most democratic of American State Constitutions. These men—and others like them —cannot be understood merely as leaders in a struggle for independence. They were the architects of a new social and economic order.

What was the situation which inspired discontent at home and which led to the establishment of a new order? We must content ourselves with a few broad generalizations.

Everywhere in the American colonies of the eighteenth century there had grown up sectional and class divisions, and these largely coincided. Along the Atlantic seaboard—in towns like Boston, Salem, New York, Philadelphia, New Bern and Charleston, or on the banks of the Connecticut, the Hudson, the Schuylkill, the James, the Roanoke, the Edisto—lived the ruling classes.

These were merchants, the landed gentry, the shippers, the lawyers, the government officials, the clergy of the established churches. They dominated the colonial assemblies—where they were over-represented—controlled the courts, owned a large part of the land, worshiped in the proper churches, were served by slaves or indentured servants, and set the social and cultural standards in their communities. They had long been accustomed to running things their own way—and for their own benefit.

And along the frontier, from Maine to Georgia—in the hill country of New England, in the valley of the Schoharie and the Susquehanna and even of the turbulent Monongahela, down the great Valley of Virginia and along the upper reaches of the Pee Dee and the Broad—there had come into existence a new society. These were the poor people, the small farmers, indentured servants who had served their time, apprentices who had run away, German redemptioners, Scotch-Irish who squatted on the lands of the Penns or of the Granvilles.

They were dissenters for the most part, worshiping in strange churches, harkening gladly to Whitefield and Tennant and Davies. They didn't own slaves and disliked the slave-holding gentry of the East. They were familiar with the war-whoop of the Indian and defended the frontier while well-protected Quakers made a profession of pacifism and tidewater planters quarreled about appropriations. They were under-represented in the colonial assemblies, ignored in appointments to office, denied access to land and to markets. They, too, had a program, but it had little to do with far-distant Parliament or George III. They wanted free land, freedom of worship, easy money, defense against Indians and their due share of political power.

There was, to be sure, a third element, small but powerful. These were the town dwellers, the seamen and wharfingers and carpenters and laborers and apprentices and tradesmen of the rising cities. These were Sam Adams's men and Franklin's— propertyless, unenfranchised, unrepresented, ready for a riot or a war, the Liberty Boys whom the Oliver Wiswells of the time regarded with such contempt.

By the Seventeen Seventies the West and the underprivileged townsmen were ripe for revolt. Some outbreaks had already taken place. In the Carolinas the Regulators took arms against intolerable neglect and oppression and, at Alamance, suffered defeat. In Virginia the men of the western waters were rallying behind Henry and the young Jefferson in an effort to wrest control of the government from the tidewater Old Guard. In Pennsylvania only the intervention of Franklin saved Philadelphia from attack by the Paxton Boys, while on the great Hudson River estates agrarian revolts were turning into open war. New England was seething with restlessness, and its safety-valve, Vermont, was saved from New York and New Hampshire land speculators only by the determination of the Green Mountain Boys.

Here, then, was the situation in the American Colonies on the eve of the War for Independence. That war played into the hands of the democratic elements in most of the American colonies. It afforded an opportunity for the realization of many of the democratic ideals and practices espoused by the West.

How did it do this? In the first place, the seaboard groups could not carry on war without the support of the numerous backcountry elements, and that support had to be bought by concessions. These concessions were written into the new Constitutions and laws of most of the States. In the second place, many of the members of the upper classes—government officials, lawyers, great landowners, Anglican clergy, wealthy merchants—sided with the mother country and thereby lost not only their offices and influence but their property as well.

Thus the great estates of the Penns, the Fairfaxes and the Granvilles were confiscated and sold to small farmers, while in New York millions of acres of loyalist estates were turned into farms for thousands of settlers. Many of the well-to-do loyalists fled the country, altogether some 70,000 going to Canada, to the British West Indies or to the mother country. The ruling classes, thus seriously weakened by loss of numbers, of wealth and of power, were unable to resist effectively the demands of the underprivileged. And, in the third place, a war fought on the theory that men are equal, that men make government, and that government derives authority from the consent of the governed, necessarily carried with it the application of those theories to the domestic situation.

How, then, were the theories of the Declaration of Independence applied, how were the principles of the Revolution actualized? Let us look first at the doctrine that government comes from below, that men can make or unmake governments. Here, if anywhere, is the essence of democracy. But this doctrine had been doctrine merely—an admirable theory, but as yet unrealized.

It remained for Americans of this Revolutionary era to give reality to this theory. This was achieved by the institution of the constitutional convention.

We take the constitutional convention so completely for granted that we do not always appreciate its significance. It is, in fact, revolution legalized. For centuries men had grappled with the problem how to get rid of tyrannous government, and they had found only one answer: force.

This resort to force was known as the right of revolution, and to it Jefferson appealed in the Declaration of Independence. But the constitutional convention discovered a legal and peaceful method of altering or abolishing old government and instituting new government. The method was simplicity itself. Voters chose delegates to meet in convention; this convention was specifically authorized to draw up a constitution; the constitution, before it could go into effect, was submitted to the vote of the people. This is the way the people of Massachusetts and New Hampshire instituted new governments during the Revolutionary War, and it is the way the people of all the American States have made or amended their fundamental laws ever since.

This great democratic institution was worked out, it will be seen, in the States. And the making, or the remaking, of Constitutions in the States enabled Americans to actualize other ideas set forth in the Declaration of Independence. Thus the principle that the right to life, liberty and the pursuit of happiness is inalienable was written into the Bills of Rights of State Constitutions generally.

Thus, too, the doctrine that the end of government is to serve the welfare and happiness of men was translated into reality. First came political reforms. With the ejection of loyalists and discrediting of conservatives, the more liberal elements took over many of the State Governments. Under-represented groups were given more adequate representation in State Legislatures and, in some cases, the basis of suffrage was broadened.

Once this had been achieved, democratic reforms followed. Old privileged forms of land ownership went by the board, and the confiscation of loyalist estates and of royal proprietary lands together with the opening up of the West gave a broader economic basis to social democracy.

Slavery, which scandalized the principle of equality, was challenged and in some places destroyed. Vermont did away with it at once; other States, like Massachusetts and New York, inaugurated a process of gradual emancipation. In the South the peculiar institution was so firmly entrenched that efforts of liberals like Jefferson to eradicate it were unavailing, but even here there was cessation of the slave trade, provision for manumission, and support for excluding it from the Northwest Territory.

This, then, is the real Revolution. It was not just a war, not even just an achievement of independence. It was a great creative era in history. It was attended by warfare and suffering, by violence and destruction, by blood and tears. But these things passed away. What remained is what counts. For out of the Revolution came a Federal union, a new colonial system, a philosophy of democracy and the institutionalization of that philosophy in the constitutional convention, a broader distribution of property and with it a broader social equality, the theory and practice of religious freedom, the beginnings of the abolition of slavery.

It is perhaps not surprising that the Oliver Wiswells of that day did not see what was going on, did not realize that the foundations were being laid for the great nation and the great democratic society that has since come into being. It would, however, be astonishing if, a century and a half later, the descendants of the Oliver Wiswells should suffer from the same blindness.

Nation or States—
To Which the Power?

by James Truslow Adams

CONGRESS IS MEETING in special session to consider measures which involve the pressing issue of centralization of government. Regional planning, crop control, wages and hours, even government reorganization—all these questions are tied to the problem of whether there shall be more or less centralization of power at Washington. Not since the period of the adoption of the Constitution, and that immediately preceding the Civil War, have Americans had to consider so searchingly the fundamentals of their whole system of government. That government, in the 150 years since its adoption, has, among other factors, permitted the people of the United States to expand from a nation of a little over 4,000,000 to one of 130,000,000.

It has met the problems of an enormous increase in territory and of a completely altered economic and social world in spite of what the President calls the "lags" in judicial decisions. In a world tortured with religious, racial and national strifes, it has enabled millions of all races to live at peace within our borders. Europe has some twenty or so sovereign independent States and

From the *New York Times Magazine*, November 21, 1937, copyright © 1937, 1965 by The New York Times Company.

the United States is made up of forty-eight, but think of the difference in the way the European States live with one another and the way the American States do. It is worth considering both how the result has been achieved among ourselves and the present effort to alter the means by which that result has been obtained.

Our original thirteen States, if not hostile, were at least extremely jealous of one another. They had strongly conflicting interests. They decided, however, to confederate into one union. The essence of the form of the federal system which they devised is the division of powers among the departments of the Federal Government, between that government and the States, and between all of these and the people themselves. Conditions change, and there has been going on for many decades a slow but steady centralization of powers in the Federal Government. Nevertheless, we have never witnessed before in our history such a concentrated attack all along the line as President Roosevelt has made on the American system as we have hitherto understood it.

We need not here rehearse all the details, which are well known, but may note some of the aspects of the struggle. After four years of many measures proposed or adopted, it appears that the aim of the President is twofold: First, to concentrate power in the hands of the Federal Government as opposed to the States, and, second, within the Federal Government itself to concentrate power in the hands of the Executive. I do not believe, in the year or two during which Mr. Roosevelt was being groomed for the Presidency, that he at all envisaged his present goal. His speeches at the time all point in the opposite direction. They indicate that he was devoted to the doctrine of "States' Rights," and believed that concentration of power in Washington was something to be avoided and curbed as far as possible.

But two things happened. The President took office in the midst of an appalling depression, which seemed to make it necessary that unusual temporary powers be conferred on the Chief Executive. Moreover, Mr. Roosevelt, instead of being in the Governor's Mansion in Albany, was in the White House. The love of power grows by what it feeds on. As Governor, Mr. Roosevelt derived power from the power of the State; as President, from concentration of power at Washington. Much of the change in the President has probably been due to this shift and is wholly unconscious.

Again, all sorts of fascinating experiments for the good of the people, as he saw it, were opened up to him by his unofficial advisers—experiments which could be tried quickly, and by himself, only by discarding the old American system. He wished to be the author of the experiments. He wished to secure their benefits to the people at once, "Now, now, now," as he said in one speech. The immediacy of experiment overshadowed, eclipsed, in fact, the long-range view of proper constitutional development. It was, in part, the same psychology that led the Republican President Theodore Roosevelt into his mistake of the Colombian-Panama imbroglio so that the canal could be dug during his own Administration—a mistake which cost the country dear in both money and honor. I think that helps to explain the President and his contradictions.

Relief called for temporary concentration of hitherto un-dreamed-of powers in the hands of the Executive. The old-fashioned "patronage" of the Presidents dwindled to insignificance as compared with the ten billions or so this President has had to spend on relief. States, counties, cities and towns reached out eager hands. Twenty-five per cent of the citizens, it has been said, at one time were being supported in whole or in part by Federal money.

There were also the other enormous powers, such as control over the gold content of the dollar, over tariffs, over the two billions of gold in the stabilization fund, and so on. The need for creating jobs, working together with the farm problem, the soil problem, flood control, the public utilities problem and all the rest, seemed to make necessary, in the President's opinion, that very concentration of control by Washington which he had himself for years deplored.

The emergency powers came to be looked upon, not as something to be used as sparingly as possible and relinquished at the earliest moment, but as powers which should belong permanently to the Federal Government. Little by little we have witnessed this silent revolution going on, until it looks as though Aaron's rod would supplant all the others. Local and State pride has broken down under the pressure of necessity or greed.

The Federal Government has been invading the sphere of the States in every direction—education, road building, local park improvement and so on through the long list. Such experiments at the TVA and others broke down State lines and while making the States almost negligible as sovereign units have enormously increased the power of the Federal Government. It all fits into one picture—the breakdown of Federal Government and the creation of one of the strongest centralized governments in the world.

What is the Federal system which the President either desires or is willing to destroy? In some respects ours is unique in history. Ordinarily, federal governments had been weak because they had been essentially leagues of independent and sovereign States.

When ours was formed there were thirteen such independent commonwealths, all jealous of one another. Owing not only to their jealousy but also to the distances, difficulties of communication and local differences of habits and needs among them, it was impossible that they should all be ruled by a consolidated government in Washington. The problem was how to avoid the dangers of consolidation and also the inherent weakness of all previous federal governments.

Those who solved this problem made a new contribution to political philosophy. It had always been considered that sovereignty could reside only in government and in one government. From time to time subjects, such as the Barons at Runnymede, won "liberties" from the sovereign. The men who drew up our Constitution had a wholly new idea. They knew the weakness of federalism and the dangers of concentrated power, so they divided powers between the Federal Government and the States, and for the first time divided sovereignty. They made citizens directly subject to the Federal Government in respect to the powers it possessed, and to their individual States in respect to the powers they retained.

It was a bold experiment, but it worked. Certain powers were given, and others denied, to the central government; still others were retained by or denied to the States; but a vast reservoir of powers was retained by the people themselves to be exercised, when the need arose, by the constitutional process of amendment. Because either the central government or the States might oppress the people or grasp after too great power, it was provided that the process of amendment might be initiated either in the Federal Government through Congress or in the States themselves through the demands of their Legislatures for the presentation of amendments.

The founders of the Constitution realized the danger of centralized power in a vast and varied nation. They also realized the danger from the States, such as that which eventuated in the Civil War. For this reason they divided ultimate sovereignty into three parts.

But they also realized two other things. One was that they could not foresee all future conditions, and so they provided for the amendment of the Constitution through the sovereignty of the people. The other was that if it was dangerous to trust to the non-abuse of sovereignty by either central or State governments, so it was also dangerous to trust to the sudden decision of the people made in the heat of a political election, with regard to changes in the fundamental laws and rights of the nation as distinct from ordinary legislation. They left to the people the final word as to needed changes in the Constitution to meet new conditions, but provided that such word should be given only after careful consideration. Hence the system of amendments.

Such were the basic ideas of our American Federal system, new in the world at the time. It was a magnificent conception, a new form of governmental architecture. But this new form of arch required a keystone to keep it from falling, and that keystone is the Supreme Court.

In this form of government, which was designed to preserve the liberties of the people not only from tyrants but from the tyranny of ill-considered and hasty acts of the people themselves under the temporary sway of a demagogue or other dangerous influences, many disputes could arise. There was the dual citizenship of every citizen, his relations to the Federal Government and to his State; there were the relations between the central government and the State governments; and there was the balance of power among the three departments of the central government. If the structure was not to crumble there must be provided somewhere an independent power to decide controversies.

As has been well said, "neither executive officers nor Legislatures are good judges of the extent of their own powers," nor, we may add, are ambitious politicians in any country. An independent judiciary, free of political ambitions and learned in constitutional law, is the necessary balance wheel to keep the machine of Federal Government running without breakdown.

That machine has run for 150 years with the one breakdown of the Civil War, the result of which was to reinstate the system and make it more powerful than before. In that century and a half it has suffered strains and stresses such as no other newly established government of such magnitude has ever had to withstand. We have grown from a nation of about 4,000,000 to one of 130,000,000. We have spread across a land 3,000 miles wide.

We began when for transportation there were only sailing ships at sea and horses on land, when there was no steam, electricity, or any of the modern inventions. We have now lived into the machine, mass-production age of today. The original thirteen States have increased to forty-eight with possessions overseas unprovided for in the original scheme. We have had to absorb several score millions of alien people attracted to us not less by the liberties guaranteed and secured to them by our courts and our Constitution than by the possibility of gaining property, which would be worthless without the constitutional guarantees. We have preserved our individual liberties.

The division of powers and sovereignty has worked; and the

Supreme Court has worked as the balance wheel. In spite of unpopular decisions given by it at times, the people have clung to it as the bulwark of their liberties, especially those fundamental ones of freedom of religion, speech and press. The President is Commander in Chief of the army and navy. Congress holds the purse strings of the nation. State governments have their own military forces. The Supreme Court has but one official to enforce its decrees, one sole United States Marshal, but the people have accepted and obeyed its decisions. Nothing could more strongly emphasize the respect the court has won in general opinion, or the belief of the people that it is an all-essential part of the Federal system.

In different administrations the balance of power between Congress and the Executive has shifted back and forth, but there has always been the Supreme Court to maintain the liberty of the citizen in the last resort. Without the court and the rest of the Federal system I do not believe that the nation could have survived the growing pains of its history from 1789 to today.

That is the system which we have recently seen threatened with destruction by the largely decreased sovereignty of the States, by the attempt to control the Supreme Court, and by the unprecedented concentration of power in the executive department of the central government. Yet Mr. Roosevelt himself said in his last term as Governor of New York the Constitution has proved itself "the most marvelously elastic compilation of the rules of government ever written."

Is the Federal system now outmoded? I do not believe so. It is true that "the horse-and-buggy days" have given place to the automobile age, and that innumerable other changes have come in our life, many of them requiring greater control in certain spheres by the central government. Adjustments may have to be made as they have been made in the past. We may need certain amendments to the Constitution, as we have had them on an average of one every three years for the past generation.

But there is something more fundamental in government than

trying experiments in a hurry, and that is the preservation of individual liberty. By means of the American Federal system that liberty is far more likely to be preserved than by some form of highly centralized totalitarian State set up in the name of efficiency.

Because of the telephone, railroads, cars, national brands, national advertising, nation-wide business enterprises, and so on, it is undoubtedly necessary to weld the States more closely together. But for many purposes—not all—there are two ways of doing this. It can be done by the concentration of power in Washington, which will end in the destruction of the Federal system, or by voluntary cooperation among the States themselves. The first is more speedy and to those in a hurry may seem the more efficient. The second is the way of democracy, with both the advantages and disadvantages of democratic government: it is the way of liberty.

In America we have had the blueprint plans of theorists for dividing the country into administrative sections by a stroke of the pen. We have also the present powerful movement headed by the President which, in effect, would weaken the States and strengthen the Federal Government. But there is at work also the democratic way, which has gone farther than many people realize.

In New England, for example, a clearly defined natural section, there is functioning the New England Council, made up of the Governors of the six States. As a natural and almost instinctive movement this may develop into a sort of regional government for many purposes. Then there is the American Legislators Association, which has been slowly but naturally developing since 1926. It is made up of the Legislatures of all forty-eight States, with representatives of more than 7,500 State legislators and Executives. It is working more and more effectively and holds much promise for increasing the uniformity of State laws by voluntary action instead of action imposed by Washington.

Again, we have the Council of State Governments. Thirty States are already members. Others are steadily joining. At the meeting in Washington last January there were representatives from forty-five States taking part. Out of the experience already gained the prospect of ten "regions" is emerging, "each of which would serve as the operating center for the appropriate interstate commissions functioning in the vicinity" and for "all cooperative activities of States in the same region."

These three organs of government, for such they may almost be considered, have come into being in the past ten years by the democratic method. They have been a natural growth, coming from the people themselves, just as came gradually our political parties, machines and conventions. These latter were not imposed on us all at once by blueprint planners but grew to fit our needs and our particular political ways.

No doubt there is need of greater coordination between the States and the central government and among the States themselves. The situation is somewhat similar to that with respect to property. As civilization becomes more complex, forms of property which have been purely personal become tinged with a public interest, and their use has to be considered in the light of the good of the whole community instead of merely that of the owner. Likewise, certain legislation, previously wholly local, becomes tinged with a national interest and has to be considered in a new aspect.

There are, however, two ways of meeting the need, as the American Legislators Association points out. "The Federal Government may take over the major functions of the States and build up an organization from the top down," or "the States may retain many of their major functions and build up an organization from the bottom up." For example, the Federal Government could take over the Port of New York and run it for the benefit of New York and New Jersey, or those States, as they have done, could get together and run it jointly. So with the regional power schemes of the President and many other matters. That, it seems to me, is the proper way wherever feasible. Centralization, if it has to proceed, should go as slowly, and not as rapidly, as possible.

Why do I believe so profoundly in the Federal system? I may begin by quoting the words of President Roosevelt, uttered a few short years ago. "The preservation of home rule by the States," he said, "is not a cry of jealous Commonwealths seeking their own aggrandizement. . . . It is a fundamental necessity if we are to remain a truly united nation."

And again, after saying that there were no master minds "so godlike in their ability" that they could plan for the whole country, he added that "to bring about government by oligarchy masquerading as democracy it is fundamentally essential that practically all authority and control be centralized in our national government. The individual authority of our States must first be destroyed except in mere minor matters of legislation."

The President also warned us some months ago that already he had built up instruments of power in Washington which, beneficent in his hands, would, in the hands of possible others, "provide shackles for the liberties of the people." Since then he has asked for more and more powers.

I have watched close at hand and in Europe the way dictatorships develop. There is a crisis. A leader seizes or is given unusual powers. The crisis may pass, but the leader and the powers remain. The legislatures become mere shadow puppets or disappear. Then the courts go. All personal liberties go, and the complete dictator emerges, whether at the beginning he intended to be a dictator or not. Once he is on the road, circumstances may force his hand.

That is the reason why I do not wish to abandon the old American Federal system, and I believe that the President's own repeated warnings are correct. If we destroy the powers of the States or the division of powers in Washington, we open the way, as he told us, to a masquerade of democracy. If we give up the Federal system, with its necessary unit of an independent judiciary and with its balance of powers to control the central executive, we shall feel those shackles on our personal liberties which the President has told us are ready if the instruments of power he has created fall into the wrong hands in some election. That is why I am so bitterly opposed, not to the President's humanitarian objectives, but to his avowed methods of attaining them.

Nation or the States—Which Shall Dominate?

by Henry Steele Commager

PRESIDENT ROOSEVELT has recently reminded us that the Constitution was designed to protect the rights of majorities as well as those of minorities. It may be well to recall, too, that it was designed to create a nation, as well as to preserve States. It is not without significance that, while independence was the declaration of the thirteen United States, and the Articles of Confederation were among thirteen States, the Constitution was ordained by "the people of the United States," and its first object was "to form a more perfect Union."

This object was attained by a new political device—the division of powers between governments. All powers necessary and proper to the general welfare were allocated to the National Government, all others lodged in the States. The chief problem which faced the framers of the Constitution was that of the wise and expedient division of these powers. It was all very well to agree that powers of a general nature should be given to the general government; those of a local character to the State governments. But what were the powers of a general nature?

Was the regulation of taxation, foreign and domestic commerce, Western lands, Indian affairs, the proper task of the central government? Was the control of suffrage, education, labor, morals, social institutions, the proper task of the local governments? Every one agreed that some government had to exercise power over these matters, but it was not easy to draw the line of division. British statesmen had attempted to make such a division and had ended up by insisting that Parliament "had, hath, and of right ought to have, full power and authority to make laws and statutes . . . in all cases whatsoever."

This, obviously, was no solution; it was an admission of complete inability to arrive at a solution. The fathers of the Revolution had tried, in the Articles of Confederation, to work out a different and more satisfactory division of powers. Their plan was closer to realities than that of Parliament, but it was not successful because it did not grant to the central government essential powers of a general character. The framers of the Constitution succeeded where their predecessors had failed because they worked out a division of powers in accordance with realities.

The moral which derives from this chapter of our history is inescapable. Federalism—the division of powers between governments—is not a conclusion of a syllogism but a product of experience. It is not the recognition of a theory but the acknowledgment of facts. The question of which government is best prepared to exercise governmental powers and undertake administrative responsibilities is to be answered not by reference to some preconceived pattern of ideas but by reference to actualities. Whenever men have failed to appreciate this elementary axiom, there has been trouble. Englishmen failed to appreciate it, and discontented Americans disrupted the empire. Americans in 1777 failed to realize it, and all but lost the Revolutionary War as a result. Southern statesmen, in the decade before the Civil War, forgot it, and their blindness to the growth of nationalism had catastrophic consequences.

Yet some commentators would have us believe that federalism

is something fixed and final, a law of nature, immaculate and immutable. It is, on the contrary, a rule of practice. The proper approach to the problem of federalism is not one of legal doctrine, but of sociological experiment. It is a pragmatic question, and it may be asserted that there never was a more pragmatic body than the group that framed the Constitution.

The efforts of the present Administration to extend national supervision over such matters as industry, labor, agriculture, power production, relief and similar activities have excited a good deal of trepidation and some dismay. It is well to remember that this is no new development, but merely the continuation of a process which has been under way since the beginning of the Republic, and that at every stage that process has excited similar dismay and inspired prophecies of disaster. For the causes of the growth of national power lie, of course, not in the ambitions of men but in the growth of the nation itself and the rapid development of national economic institutions.

The beginnings of that process date back to the Washington Administration, when it was found expedient to use the national power to establish a national bank and to erect a tariff that had protective features—that was designed, in short, to build up a self-sufficient nation. Washington's successors, of whatever party, were equally willing to recognize realities. It was Jefferson, often thought a doctrinaire advocate of State rights, who bought Louisiana, doubling at one stroke the national territory and giving an immense impetus to nationalism, and it was the same Jefferson who did not hesitate to use the powerful weapon of the embargo in an effort to perserve peace.

Madison had written the Virginia resolutions asserting the right of the State to nullify acts of Congress, but he did not hesitate to sign the recharter of the national bank nor the tariff of 1816. John Quincy Adams counted himself a Jeffersonian, but his plan for national improvements, national aid to science and education, marks him, too, as a far-sighted realist. Andrew Jackson, representative of frontier democracy, gave short shrift to the dialectics of State sovereignty. And the policies of these men were dictated, in every case, by a common-sense recognition of actualities.

They saw that a nation was coming into existence, a nation with a common character and common problems. They saw what rugged John Marshall put with characteristic forcefulness:

> That the United States form, for many and for most important purposes a single nation, has not yet been denied. In war we are one people. In making peace we are one and the same people. In many other respects the American people are one, and the government, which is alone capable of controlling and managing their interests in all these respects, is the government of the Union. It is their government, and in that character they have no other. America has chosen to be, in many respects, and to many purposes, a nation: and for all these purposes her government is competent. The people have declared that in the exercise of all the powers given for these objects it is supreme.

The extension of national power, then, came in response to inescapable demands. Those demands resulted in part from the expansion of the nation westward, in part from war, in part from the growth of industry, transportation, finance on a national scale. The development of federal centralization, indeed, has proceeded most rapidly since the transformation of the national economy from agricultural to industrial. For it was speedily apparent that the States could not, individually, cope with such matters as immigration, railroads, trusts and monopolies, and the exploitation of natural resources that knew no State boundaries.

In the last quarter of the nineteenth century came a recognition of the imperative necessity of national regulation of these problems. In 1882 Congress passed the first comprehensive Immigration Bill. Five years later came the Interstate Commerce Act, and in 1890 the Sherman Anti-Trust Act. Thereafter legislation empowering the Federal Government to do what the States could not do, came thick and fast. But it came, in every instance, not as a result of some intellectual conviction as to its theoretical advisability, but as a result of immediate necessity.

And it came, too, without any serious impairment of essential State rights. For the expansion of Federal jurisdiction over matters of business and industry and finance and natural resources did not involve a transfer of certain vital powers from State to Federal Government. The Federal Government entered into these fields only where the States had proved themselves impotent.

When Congress finally assumed control over immigration the States did not lose a right or a power which they had heretofore exercised, but Congress exercised a power which had lain dormant. When the Federal Government finally undertook to regulate the railroads the States were not required to surrender any privilege which was of value or utility, but Congress asserted authority in a field where the States had already proved themselves helpless. When the National Government, at long last, assumed responsibility for trusts and monopolies national in character it was merely doing what the States, in the nature of the case, were prevented from doing.

Indeed, it may be asserted that, despite the continuous growth of the power of the Federal Government, the States have not lost power, but gained it. What has happened, of course, is not a mere transfer of a fixed and constant body of powers from one governmental vessel to another, but an enormous growth of the power of all governments. The State of New York today exercises powers which would have astonished Alexander Hamilton and Thomas Jefferson alike, and the City of New York regulates the lives and businesses of its citizens in a hundred ways unknown to an earlier generation. The fact is that the growing complexity of society, the increasing vulnerability of society, has imposed new tasks and responsibilities upon all governments. That the tempo has been more rapid in the Federal and local fields is merely the result of the recognition that our problems are increasingly national rather than local in character.

The increase in government authority, then, is not cause but effect. It is an administrative recognition of a fact. The fact may be an unpalatable one, but the ability to accept facts and to accommodate laws to facts is an evidence of statesmanship. And the fact is, as Mr. Hoover recently observed, that "we are * * * in the midst of a great revolution, or perhaps a better word, a transformation, in the whole superorganization of our economic life. We are passing from a period of extremely individualistic action into a period of associational activities."

Those associational activities ignore State boundary lines, as the development of a national economy ignores State boundary lines. The size of the cotton crop of Texas intimately affects the cotton growers of South Carolina; the discount policies of New York banks must be observed by banks in Iowa and Arkansas; textile wages fixed by directors in New York determine the standard of living of workingmen in Virginia and Tennessee; corporation policies formulated under the benign auspices of Delaware laws vitally influence economy and society in Illinois and California.

Business has long recognized the national character of our economy and has adjusted itself to that situation. It is illuminating to recall, for example, that many of the NRA codes were replicas of codes of fair practice already in effect in major industries. Business has long recognized the necessity of national control of production and distribution, of national regulation of prices and wages, and has found in the maintenance of national policies stability and safety.

During the decade of the Twenties the Republican party encouraged this development, both by the negative policy of laissez-faire and by a positive policy of government support and subsidy, and the interests which are today most bitter in their denunciation of Federal centralization found these government policies unobjectionable. Federal subsidies to merchant marine, Federal subsidies to aviation, Federal support to ailing railroads and banks, inspired no awkward questions of the danger of Federal centralization. Business, in short, has no serious objection to national organization and supervision, but merely to government regulation of that organization. It has no objection to regimentation, it demands merely that it command the regiments.

The growth of Federal centralization under the New Deal has taken no new direction; it has hardly invaded new fields. But it has been inspired by a different philosophy. It has advanced the principle that business activities vitally affecting the national economy be under the control of the nation. It has insisted that if there is to be regimentation, the representatives of the nation, not of business, command the regiments.

Analysis of the centralizing policies of the New Deal confirms this generalization. The most notable examples of centralization of power have been the NRA, the AAA and the TVA. The first two were voided by the Supreme Court—which has in the past been one of the most powerful agents of centralization in our political system—but it appears that they are to be revived; the third has, so far, stood the test of constitutionality. All three involve an extension of national jurisdiction over areas heretofore unclaimed; all three inspire understandable apprehension for the maintenance of the Federal system.

In each case the argument behind the extension of Federal control was that of necessity. In each case the Administration took the position that the problem involved was national in scope and that only the National Government could solve it. The NRA, it will be recalled, was designed to meet a "national emergency" and its particular objectives were all concerned with the "general welfare." Its effort to fix prices, wages, hours of labor and to regulate industrial practices was justified by the belief that State and local regulation of these matters had proved ineffective and that private control had proved futile.

The Supreme Court, in the Schechter case, did not deny the validity of the argument, only the propriety of the application, holding that the sale of "sick chickens" did not vitally affect national economy or justify the extension of commerce power over that particular business. But two years later, in the Wagner case, the court took a broader position. "We are asked to shut our eyes," said the Chief Justice, "to the plainest facts of our national life and to deal with the question of direct and indirect effects in an intellectual vacuum. * * * When industries organize themselves on a national scale, making their relation to interstate commerce the dominant factor in their activities, how can it be maintained that their industrial labor relations constitute a forbidden field into which Congress may not enter?"

And a brief reference to the census figures will reveal that most important industries have organized themselves on a national scale, making State control highly impracticable. In 1933, 594 corporations owned 53 per cent of the corporate wealth of the country. One-tenth of 1 per cent of manufacturing corporations owned 46 per cent of the total corporate assets; slightly over 1 per cent of the utility corporations owned over four-fifths of utility corporation assets. The three largest automobile manufacturers made nine-tenths of all automobiles; the four largest tobacco companies produced over nine-tenths of all cigarettes; four companies owned over one-half the copper resources of the country; eight corporations owned three-fourths of the anthracite coal; five companies produced one-third of all the oil; one corporation dominated the production of nickel and another the production of aluminum.

The situation which appeared to justify regulation of agricultural production was a different one. Farming suffered not from individual monopoly but from individualism. Ever since the reconstruction years farmers had attempted to organize in their own interests, and the history of the Granger, the Alliance and the Farmer-Labor movements reveals the ineffectiveness of such voluntary organization. Nor has State control of production or State regulation of soil and water and forest exploitation proved successful. Indeed, such regulation is so impracticable that it has never even been tried in any comprehensive fashion.

The experience of American farmers in the past, the experience of governments abroad, all indicated that the National Government was the only one competent to cope with the problems of production and soil control. The Republican Administration recognized this and attempted to exercise some such national control through the Agricultural Marketing Act of 1929. The act was a lamentable failure. Mr. Roosevelt's plan, the AAA, involved a franker and fuller recognition of national responsibility and a far greater degree of centralization of power, and by every pragmatic test it succeeded where other plans had failed.

The Supreme Court, in the Hoosac Mills case, held the act void as an improper invasion of the powers of the States. "The decisions of this court," said Mr. Justice Butler, "will be searched in vain for any suggestion that there exists in the Constitution the authority whereby every provision and every fair implication from that instrument may be subverted, the independence of the individual States obliterated and the United States converted into a central government exercising controlled police power in every State of the Union." But Mr. Justice Stone replied that this opinion "hardly rises to the dignity of argument," and warned his colleagues against a "tortured construction of the Constitution." Where judges confessed such differences on the meaning of the Constitution, laymen might well be confused.

The question of water-power control is equally a question of fact, to be determined by pragmatic, not theoretical, tests. The Tennessee Valley Act recognized the artificiality of State boundary lines and set up an authority with jurisdiction in seven States. Such an authority might conceivably have been created by inter-state compacts, such as the Colorado River compact. The fact is that the States took no action in the matter, and the Federal Government stepped in to undertake what States were unprepared to do and private capital unwilling to do. That the objectives of the TVA—improvement of navigation, production of nitrate and of power, agricultural rehabilitation, soil control, social re-generation—are of national concern few will deny. That the National Government controls the most effective instruments for attaining those objectives would appear to be clear. That national action in the matter seriously impairs any essential rights of States or any essential liberties of individuals has yet to be proved.

The true principle of federalism is that it be adjusted to realities.

The line of division between State and central governments is a pragmatic, not a syllogistic, line. Those powers which can best be exercised by State governments should be left with State governments; those powers which can best be exercised by the central government should be allocated to the central government. This was the philosophy which animated the framers of the Constitution in 1787; it is the philosophy which permeates the decisions of John Marshall; it is the philosophy behind the growth of nationalism in the United States in the last three-quarters of a century.

But it must be remembered that the determination of the allocation of powers rests not alone upon considerations of efficiency but even more emphatically upon considerations of larger social welfare and liberty. If the growth of Federal power should threaten the liberties of men under government, that growth should be stopped. It is essential, therefore, that the Federal Government and the men who staff it should be animated by a disinterested regard for national welfare, that they do not encourage the development of a bureaucracy, that they guard against the temptations of abuse of power for personal or party purpose, and that they beware even the appearance of dictatorial powers.

Critics of the New Deal have warned us that the growth of Federal power threatens the rights of the States and the liberty of citizens and that it violates the integrity of the American Federal system. They call for a return to federalism as it was in Washington's day, or in Lincoln's. They extol the Federal experiment of 1787 but are unwilling to permit experimentation to go further. They celebrate the originality and audacity of the authors of the Federal system, but lament the originality and boldness of the architects of modern America. They admit that the federalism of 1787 was a realistic adaptation of means to ends, a sensible adjustment of theory to fact, but they decry further adaptation and adjustment for our own generation.

They argue—and we have only to turn to recent Supreme Court decisions for such arguments—that the maintenance of State rights is an end in itself.

In the face of such arguments it is refreshing to turn to John Marshall's famous conclusion in the case of Gibbons v. Ogden:

"Powerful and ingenious minds, taking as postulates that the powers expressly granted to the government of the Union are to be contracted, by construction, into the narrowest possible compass, and that the original powers of the States are to be retained, if any possible construction will retain them, may, by a course of well-digested but refined and metaphysical reasoning founded on these premises, explain away the Constitution of our country, and leave it a magnificent structure, indeed, to look at, but totally unfit for use. They may so entangle and perplex the understanding as to obscure principles which were thought quite plain, and induce doubts where, if the mind were to pursue its own course, none would be perceived. In such a case, it is peculiarly necessary to recur to safe and fundamental principles."

Part 4

THE OTHER SIDE

THE REVOLUTION has an immediacy for Americans which often limits their perspective and causes them to ignore its momentous effects upon those who lost the war. The Revolution disrupted the British Empire, successfully challenged British premises, and forced a reconstitution of the British system at home and abroad.

R. L. Duffus examines eighteenth-century English attitudes toward events across the Atlantic and finds a sharp division in British society. Opponents of the Revolution—the Tories—at first despised colonials and later feared the consequences for England of their actions. Those who supported the Revolution—the Whigs—apparently did so because of ideological principles involved, but one may wonder how many were simply members of the "loyal opposition." Certainly few attacked the King directly for his American policies; instead they aimed their animus at the King's ministers who misled him.

Modern British popular attitudes are explored by James Truslow Adams, who finds a marked lack of concern or interest in the American Revolution. Americans are far more sensitive than

Englishmen about the breakup of the Empire. Adams attributes this to the fact that the English, having imbibed the Whig tradition for so long, accept the policies of the 1760's and 1770's as their mistake. Moreover, the Englishmen's perspective is much longer. The Revolution was but one incident in their two-thousand-year history, and but one loss amidst many victories. Lack of British concern may deflate some American egos, but it does remind us that the American Revolution was only a small part of an intermittent Anglo-French war that lasted from 1688 to 1815. Britain's ultimate victory over Napoleon dimmed the significance of its loss of America.

Professor Keith Feiling, a noted Tory scholar, examines British historical treatment of the Revolution. Distressed by the obvious Whig bias in scholarly and popular histories, he admits that no Englishman could properly write a Tory account of the Revolution. Rather, the initiative for a restoration of balance must come from American scholars, for only they can chip away at the assumption that all virtue emanated from Americans and all vice derived from Englishmen.

As the British Viewed Our Revolution

by R. L. Duffus

PREMIER MACDONALD the other day gently twitted the historians on the fallibility of their art, observing that if the story of the American Revolution had been written more largely by Tories it might now appear in quite a different light. Perhaps the Prime Minister had not read all the British historians of the Revolution. If, for example, he had dipped into Volume I of "The Cambridge History of the British Empire" he might have found Mr. Cecil Headlam taking some nasty cracks at the Colonists and arriving at the conclusion that "George III may have been narrow-minded and obstinate, but he was faithful to the ideas of kingship and the interests of the empire as he conceived them."

On the whole, however, Mr. MacDonald was justified in asserting that it was the Whig version of the fracas between America and the mother country which has prevailed, not only in the United States but in Great Britain. This is not entirely unnatural, since historians, for the sake of their own peace of mind, are driven to find reasonableness in the things that actually occurred. It is only in comparatively recent years that some of them have

From the *New York Times Magazine,* August 2, 1931, copyright © 1931, 1959 by The New York Times Company.

turned to exposing the unreasonableness of certain past events, and the new doctrines have not yet penetrated either the school curricula or the popular mind.

But Premier MacDonald's remarks do suggest that, without entering into the question of the correctness of any new doctrines about the Revolution, we inquire as to what the British thought about it while it was actually going on. It is on contemporary opinions quite as much as on contemporary facts that the historians of any period have to draw.

Most of us learned from our school histories that, although the King and his Ministers, a considerable portion of the aristocracy, and all the job-holders who wanted to keep their jobs were anti-American, the great masses of the British people were with the Colonists. There is certainly some truth in this statement, but it is certainly not 100 per cent true.

Let us glance for a moment at some of the outstanding personalities and arguments on the anti-American side. A most conspicuous figure was the learned Dr. Samuel Johnson. So bigoted was Johnson on this subject that even the admiring Boswell was moved to stand out against him. At the beginning, early in 1775, the lexicographer was of the opinion that "our government has been precipitant and severe in the resolutions taken against the Bostonians," though he had declared some years earlier that the Americans were "a race of convicts and ought to be thankful for anything we allow them short of hanging." Later he thundered against the Colonists in a pamphlet entitled "Taxation No Tyranny," which he admitted to Boswell had been "revised and curtailed" by certain members of the Tory party. There can be no doubt that Johnson was somewhat influenced by the pension granted him by George III "as the reward of his literary merit," and not much doubt that the very violence of his expressions covered an uneasy conscience.

Another literary man who might conceivably have had a guilty conscience was Edward Gibbon, author of the "Decline and Fall of the Roman Empire." Gibbon, at first inclined to favor the Americans, accepted an office under the Tory Ministry and changed sides almost overnight. McPherson, author of the pseudo-saga, "Ossian," secretly received a pension of £500 a year from the King and dutifully produced a pamphlet called "The Right of Great Britain Asserted." John Wesley, who was still in sympathy with the Church of England, supported the King, and many of the early Methodists were with him.

If we read the summaries of the Parliamentary debates and other public expressions of opinion, as recorded, for instance, in Dodsley's Annual Register, we find that the anti-American party was not only strong but expressed itself with considerable vigor. The King's spokesmen in the Commons argued that "the punishment of a worst sort of traitors, such as Hancock and his crew, might be sufficient to teach the rest their duty," held that "the boasted union of the Colonies would dissolve the moment Parliament showed itself resolved on measures of vigor and severity," and maintained that the Americans "were neither soldiers nor could be made so, being naturally of a pusillanimous disposition and utterly incapable of any sort of order or discipline." They added that the rebels were "too ungrateful, too refractory and too incorrigible to be won by kindness." As the war proceeded many came to feel, as the well-disposed editor of The Register himself admits, that "whoever was right in the beginning, the American insolence deserved chastisement at present."

The Register added, in 1777: "A majority of the people gave at least a kind of tacit approbation to the war; but as it was not attended with national antipathy or rivalship, established enmity, or even a present competition for glory, they did not feel themselves so much interested in its success, or altogether so anxious about its consequences, as they would in those of another nature." As the war dragged on the question was even raised whether the Colonies, if successful, would not sooner or later be more powerful than the mother country; "such were the sources of wealth and power in that vast continent," it was argued, "that this small island must in a few years sink to nothing and perhaps be reduced to that most degrading and calamitous of all possible situations, the becoming a vassal to her own rebellious Colonies." Thus, from despising the Americans the Tories came in the end to fear them.

But the friends of the Colonies, though not at first as numerous in Parliament, or perhaps anywhere else in the British Isles, as their enemies, were just as vehement and in course of time more confident. They were of all sorts, the wise and the foolish, the respectable and the profligate. They included Burke, whose speech on conciliation has made thousands of school children miserable, but whose sentiments were full of nobility. They included the great Pitt, elevated to the peerage as Earl Chatham. They included the obstreperous John Wilkes, whose love of liberty and passion for notoriety were equally strong and had been equally successful in landing him in jail, in exile and in Parliament. They included some of the most influential merchants in London, Liverpool, Manchester and other cities, who saw their trade being ruined by the embargo on American shipments. They were dreadfully outspoken, both in their admiration of the Americans and in their denunciation of the men who, as the technically loyal phrase had it, were "misleading" the King.

Chatham himself went so far as to declare: "If the Ministers thus persevere in misadvising and misleading the King I will not say that they can alienate the affections of his subjects from his crown, but I will affirm that they will make the crown not worth his wearing." "Resistance to your acts," he thundered at the Commons, in a voice more powerful than was expected from a sick and aged man, "was as necessary as it was just; and your vain declarations of the omnipotence of Parliament and your imperious doctrines of the necessity of submission will be found equally incompetent to convince or enslave your fellow-subjects in America, who feel that tyranny, whether ambitioned by an individual part of the Legislature or the bodies who compose it, is equally intolerable to British subjects."

The news of Lexington and Concord led to the organization of subscriptions in London for the families of the Americans who had fallen because they "had preferred death to slavery." Petitions opposing the King's policy in the strongest terms poured in from

London itself, and from Newcastle, Bristol, Liverpool, Birmingham, Manchester, Leeds, Glasgow, Belfast and Nottingham. On Oct. 11, 1775, 1,171 "merchants and traders" of London addressed a "humble petition" to the King denouncing the war as "uncertain in the event, destructive in its consequences and the object contended for lost in the contest." On the first Independence Day, July 4, 1776, the burghers of London City, meeting in the Common Hall, requested the House of Commons to ask of his Majesty "who were the advisers of these fatal measures, who had planted Popery and arbitrary power in America, and had plunged us into a most unnatural civil war, to the subversion of the fundamental principles of English liberty, the ruin of our most valuable commerce, and the destruction of his Majesty's subjects."

We are told that General Conway described the war as "cruel, unnecessary and unnatural, calling it in plain terms a butchery of his fellow-subjects." In 1776, nineteen Lords, headed by Burke's patron, Lord Rockingham, signed a protest against the House of Lords' address in reply to the King's speech from the throne, "because we cannot, as Englishmen or Christians, or as men of common humanity, consent to the prosecution of a cruel civil war, so little supported by justice and so very fatal in its necessary consequences." The Earl of Effingham and several other prominent officers resigned their commissions in the army rather than fight against the Colonials. Though the Scotch were disposed to support the King, the Protestant Irish, with the exception of the officeholders and the gentry, were almost unanimously pro-American.

The editor of The Annual Register, which has already been quoted, opened his volume for 1775 by saying: "It indeed little becomes us to be dogmatical and decided in our opinions in the matter when the public, even on this side of the water, is so much divided and when the first names of the country have differed so greatly in their sentiments." But there is an obvious tolerance for the American point of view in this supposedly unbiased editor's pages. The Revolutionary party in the Colonies he describes as "too numerous to be bribed and too bold to be despised without danger." When each side accused the other of "atrocities" after the fights at Lexington and Concord, he sagely commented: "Civil wars produce many such charges, but we have good reason and some authority for believing that these accounts, if at all true on either side, were much exaggerated." And later, in discussing the plight of Washington's army at Valley Forge, he spoke of "the general strong disposition of the Americans to suffer all things rather than submit to force."

It is clear enough as one reads these passages, and clear still when one fits them into the contemporary political history of Great Britain itself, that the American war was as much a domestic crisis as the struggle with the Stuart Kings had been. It was not merely the power of the throne, supported by a corrupt Parliament, to rule the American Colonies that was at stake, but its power to rule England. The American Revolution was in a sense also an English revolution, though its land battles took place 3,000 miles off the English coast. The ferocity of the debates in Parliament and in the press was a product of fear. Little more than a century had passed since the English had found it necessary to behead a King. They might have done it again had not King George been forced to yield by political pressure and had not the excesses of the French Revolution, a few years after American indpendence was attained, disgusted even Burke with "democracy."

We may trace the rising tide of opposition to the King and to his American policy in the votes in Parliament. In the early years of the war the King's party won on decisive questions by such majorities as 270 to 78, 242 to 87, 232 to 83, in the House of Commons and even more decisive majorities in the House of Lords. But when the news of Yorktown reached England, late in 1781, the Ministerial majority in the Commons dropped from 220 to 179. Then General Conway arose to move "that the House would consider as enemies to his Majesty and the Country all those who should advise or by any means attempt the further prosecution of offensive war on the continent of North America for the purpose of reducing the revolted Colonies to obedience by force." The motion was carried and the war to all intents and purposes was over.

How closely public opinion followed the Parliamentary votes it is impossible to say. Because the suffrage was still limited and because elections were hopelessly corrupt there is no positive evidence as to what the people thought. The Annual Register testifies repeatedly to their apathy toward the war.

But will history ever become so nearly a science that the story of a far-reaching event like the American Revolution can be written once for all, beyond the danger of serious modification? That cerebral New England genius, Henry Adams, doubted that it could. Premier MacDonald, if his words are to be taken literally, shares the doubt. The laws of history, if they exist, are indeed hard to discover. Too often such apparent accidents as the failure of Howe to push home his victory and destroy General Washington's army after the Battle of Long Island, or the stubbornness of a single individual such as George III, seem to be decisive. Yet one heartening fact arises out of a glance at English opinion of America and Americans during and after the Revolution. The governments of the two countries have twice been at war, and once, during the struggle between North and South, nearly at war, yet it can be said that the two peoples as a whole, and particularly the more liberal and enlightened sections of the population in each country, have never been enemies.

How the British
View Our Revolution

by James Truslow Adams

IN CONSIDERING England's attitude today toward the American Revolution, I am reminded of an encounter I had some months ago with an irate Bostonian. "The English hate us," she insisted, against my mild remonstrance, "and always will. They have never forgiven us for beating them in the Revolution, and never will as long as they live." In spite of the complete absurdity of this view, it is one which I have found unexpectedly prevalent along Main Street and among more or less professionally "patriotic" Americans.

The real fact is that so far from never forgiving us for the Revolution the English have, for the most part, either forgotten it or never heard of it, and in any case are not in the slightest interested in it. That it is still a matter of contemporary interest and even emotion in America, kept alive and its flame fanned by all sorts of organized effort in the way of societies, speeches and anniversary celebrations, is attributed partly to our general oddity and difference from the old stock. The English cannot imagine

From the *New York Times Magazine,* August 23, 1931, copyright © 1931 and 1959 by The New York Times Company.

themselves becoming at all excited at this late date over their own "glorious revolution" of 1688.

One of the dangers of the present time is our easy use of abstract terms with the belief that they mean very concrete things. "England" is such a term, and quite clearly can indulge in no "attitudes." What we mean when we say England is really the vast multitude of human beings who live in England. But these vary enormously in knowledge, prejudices and opinions. If we wish to speak of "England's attitude" we shall evidently have to analyze a bit further. For our present purpose we may divide the English into the very slightly educated and the moderately well educated.

The first group embraces the largest part by far of the population. The children of the laboring and other comparatively poor classes, whose parents cannot afford what we call private schooling for them, get their education at board schools and only up to the age of 14. There is little opportunity to teach them much history, and what they get is mostly in episodic story form. It must be recalled also that the history of their own country, on which naturally the whole stress must be laid, unlike our own is 2,000 years long. In the rise of the modern empire from the days of the Britons before the landing of Julius Caesar, the affair of the lost American colonies a century and a half ago is of slight importance. It is treated—as an extremely minor episode, fairly, but makes little impression.

I asked, for example, a housemaid in a flat I had in London if she had ever heard of the American Revolution. She was a fairly well-informed girl of quick intelligence, but her immediate answer, with a rather blank look, was that she never had. On my asking her if they had ever mentioned it in school, she searched her memory and finally recalled that she had been told that America had been settled by the English but that the settlers had been unjustly taxed and had rebelled and become independent.

The great mass of board school children, who are the great mass of the nation, do not read history when they grow up and go about making their livings as maids, mechanics, farmers, factory hands or what not. Such newspapers as they read contain never an allusion to the America of 1776. I think it may safely be said that the overwhelming majority of the English people know almost nothing and care much less about our successful Revolution, which to them is the very hazy past of "history."

Let us turn now to the small minority of the well-educated. History has always occupied a very minor place in English education, even in the universities, and still does. English history, however, is taught and I have before me two of the most widely used textbooks on the subject. One of these is Gardiner's "Outline of English History from 55 B. C.," for younger children. In the list of important dates to be learned, filling several pages, the first which in any way relates to the English Colonies in America is "1775, American war began." About six pages of text are devoted to the Revolution, with complete fairness to the American side, the blame being laid chiefly on the English Ministers, who "were foolish enough to try to tax America." Speaking of Bunker Hill, it is said that the British were twice driven back with great slaughter and finally won only because the Americans had used all their ammunition.

The war, Gardiner tells the children, was a hard one for the Americans, for they were few and the English were many, but the "Americans were fighting for their own land and for their liberty." Washington is highly praised as a great man and the Americans are said to have been successful at last only because of the French alliance and the coalition of European powers against England, which is true.

The other textbook, for older students, Hassall's "Class Book of English History," treats the struggle quite as fairly, laying more stress, however, on the inevitability of eventual separation owing to distance and the gradual growing apart of the race on the two sides of the water. It speaks of ministerial blunders and attributes the final success of America to the French alliance, the incapacity of the English Generals, the ability and character of Washington, and the inferiority of the British Navy to the combined navies of the coalition. The only book for children I have found that is in any way unfair to Americans or which could lead a pupil to harbor the slightest resentment against America for the Revolution was one written more than twenty years ago by that now largely discredited jingo and hater of America, Rudyard Kipling. But today the English child of the upper classes is taught that the Americans had a just cause, fought well, and that England lost by having brought on herself a group of enemies too powerful for her.

The English, as we have said, are not much given to the study or the reading of history, but we may look at the sources of information which those graduates of the board or private schools have for further study of the Revolution to see whether they are likely to foster prejudice or hatred, as my Bostonian friend claimed. Of the older historians, those still most read are Lecky and Green. Speaking of the stamp act, Lecky notes that "from this time the English Government of America is little more than a series of deplorable blunders"; and his whole treatment of the theme is extremely fair to the American side.

Green, in his "Short History," which has been immensely popular ever since it was first published as far back as 1874 and which has perhaps been the most widely read of all English histories, is equally unprejudiced in his treatment of the American question. After the repeal of the stamp act, he says, "on both sides there remained a pride and irritability which only wise handling could have allayed; and in the present state of English policies wise handling was impossible." He praises Washington, whom he regards with "reverence," as highly as any American ever has, noting "the lofty and serene sense of duty that never swerved from its task through resentment or jealousy, that never through war or peace felt the touch of a meaner ambition, that knew no aim save that of guarding the freedom of his fellow countrymen, and no personal longing save that of returning to his own fireside when their freedom was secured."

Turning to more recent writers, we find the same tone of fairness and moderation maintained. We may dismiss Sir John Fortescue, whose unbalanced historical judgments are well understood in England, and whose almost insane dislike of all Colonials falls on the Australians and others of the present day as well as upon the American of the past. The attitude taken by Wells in his popular "Outline of History" is indicated by his chapter heading, "Civil War is Forced Upon the Colonies." Egerton, in his "British Colonial Policy," says that the English politicians caused the Revolution to become inevitable, and in his later book, "The American Revolution," he analyzes with sympathy and understanding the deeper underlying causes.

Ramsay Muir, in his "History of the British Commonwealth," says that although the Colonists had a hard case in law or logic, they were fundamentally right. "They felt," he adds, "and rightly felt, that they were defending one of the essentials of self-government, for the whole constitutional history of England taught the lesson that the control of the purse is the foundation of political liberty."

Sir Otto Trevelyan, in his four volumes on "The American Revolution," adopts the American point of view to such an extent as perhaps to be unfair to his own countrymen. Innes, in his popular four-volume "History of England," is completely fair in his presentation of the war, and blames the politicians for having got things into such a position that the British Government could not retreat and that "the Colonies could not submit even to the new taxes without surrendering their whole case, or admitting that they were not strong enough to stand up for their rights."

One of the last writers, Wingfield-Stratford, in his big "History of British Civilization," writes in much the vein of the others, and speaking of such wish as there was on the part of the general public to beat America as the war progressed says that "at best it was pride, at worst sheer cupidity, the desire for the loaves and fishes of the Colonial trade." As a result of defeat, he adds, the old ideal of an empire based only on business ties died, and liberty won a wider field.

Such is the background of information that the Englishman, either as immature student or mature reader, finds on the subject of the Revolution. I have not picked any of these books because of their treatment, but taken them all at haphazard—school texts or scholarly histories—merely as the most widely used and read in their fields. There is hardly a source of instruction that does not teach the Englishman that the very difficult problem of empire was in 1776 not solved by his statesmen of the time, who bungled badly; that the Americans had a just case, and that under the conditions war was practically inevitable; that the Americans were forced into their position, played fair, fought well, and won by means of alliances. The truth, often forgotten by our own super-patriots, is well understood in England that "the War of American Independence ended as a war of Britain against half the world," and the Englishman knows that he was not beaten by us Americans alone.

We pay little attention to military events after the surrender at Yorktown in 1781, but the English histories naturally go on for another two years with the story of the struggle England was waging against France, Spain and others in many parts of the world, until beaten by superior force with which we Americans at that time were having nothing to do. In the Revolution, as in the War of 1812, we were fighting solely against England, whereas in each case she was fighting against a whole pack of nations at once. We think in each case of winning against her, but in each case she thinks of us as only one among many who were set on her at once. She does not resent being beaten by us, because, quite truly, it never occurs to her that she was. There is no question but that, as Washington himself admitted in pleading for haste, we should have been beaten and the Revolution would have collapsed had France not joined us against England, to be followed by other nations.

Occasionally in the histories one gets the point of view that it was unfortunate that, owing to the mutual jealousies among the Colonies, they could not agree on any united policy. This, it is said, would have involved a solution of part of the problem by evolving a system of self-taxation and some sort of contribution to the cost of the war which had won Canada and freed the

Colonists from the French danger. This is the nearest approach ever made to putting the blame on the American side. The note more often struck is found in the words of the most popular of present-day writers of history for English readers, the younger Trevelyan:

"It was well that America was made. It was tragic that the making could only be effected by a war with Britain. The parting was perhaps inevitable at some date and in some form, but the parting in anger, and still more the memory of that moment's anger fondly cherished by America as the starting-point of her history, have had consequences that we rue to this day."

There is thus almost nothing in what the Englishman is taught or reads that would lead him to form any feelings of resentment about an affair in what he considers almost ancient history. In all my contacts with English people of all grades I have never found the slightest trace of any feeling of the sort. Some English people like Americans and some detest them heartily, but both of these sentiments derive from present-day policies, contacts with stray tourists, pro- or anti-American sentiments expressed regularly in the journals these people happen to read, or what not. I come back to my original statement that most English men and women know practically nothing of the American Revolution and do not care one whit about it.

The contrast with ourselves is striking, and is hinted at in the quotation just given from Trevelyan. All nations like to feel that they have a glorious past and to recite the deeds of their heroes of old. The histories of the European peoples are long, vastly long, and have been so full of characters and events as to leave little room for lasting hates. It is only recent quarrels, like the Franco-German War of 1870, that continue to cast malign shadows.

The world moves. European diplomacy and wars and commerce have crossed and recrossed in all corners of the world. The European past was very complex. On the same page in Hassall, for example, on which the English schoolboy finds the beginning of the Revolution he has had to learn about the new alignment of the European powers after 1763, the partition of Poland, the dispute over the Falkland Islands, the doings of Warren Hastings in India, the new method of governing that dependency, and the effect of the new royal marriage act. The American affair is only one of the innumerable tangles in the skein of history which wove the story of his own country in with those of all the others.

A hundred and fifty years ago England lost some colonies, but since then she gained so many more and the new empire became so much greater than the old that that eighteenth-century incident is hardly worth recalling. For 125 years after that, and even more, as contrasted with the importance for an Englishman of what was happening in Europe, India and the East, Africa and elsewhere, there was little for him to bother about in the history of the United States. It was a new and rapidly growing country, but its self-chosen aloofness from all European affairs, its comparatively modest contributions to the literature and arts of the world, all made it rather negligible to Englishmen building a new empire and busy with problems of European balance of power, and those of dominion over palm and pine. This was entirely natural. How much does any one of us know about the history of new countries—Australia, for example, or even our next-door neighbor, Canada, with a population three times as great as ours was when we disappeared from the interest of Britain in cutting the only ropes that bound us to her?

On the other hand, our own history is short. We do not go back to the mistiness of B. C. and have no half-legendary heroes. We are comparatively of yesterday, whether we choose to start with the landfall of Columbus or the settlement at Jamestown. As an independent nation we have to begin with the revolt against England. We have been extremely self-centered. Between the War of 1812 and the Spanish War we have hardly to cross our frontiers even in thought to tell the story of national development. There have been no constant contacts with problems in all parts of the world and with other nations to lessen the comparative importance in historical perspective of the few great events in our century and a half of independence. They stand out stark and naked, each with a spot-light thrown on it.

The Revolution is our romance of the past. It is our legend and our saga. It has to do duty with us for the thousand years or so which other nations possess to read and dream about, but which we amputated on that first Fourth of July.

Perhaps, in some Freudian fashion, because our past is so short we make more of it than any other nation does. We have become the most historically self-conscious of any people I know. For all these reasons the American Revolution has been burned into the American brain. Those engaged in such constant contemplation of it in America seem to think that there must be as constant a resentment about it in England. But it is the simple truth that England has forgotten all about their enemies in the Revolution for the most part and is wholly living in 1931.

As the American Revolution Appears in British Histories

by Keith Feiling

SPEAKING TO an Anglo-American conference of historians, J. Ramsay MacDonald, the British Prime Minister, said:

"There are great misunderstandings regarding British colonial policy in North America in the seventeenth and eighteenth centuries, because our historians have had a Whig bias. A writer with a Whig bias did us an injustice, but if this history had been written with a Tory bias, no one would have believed it, so we have had to wait until a scientific historian appeared in America itself."

Even the best informed politicians seem to think of historians as lonely men living in seclusion, each with his bee, or bias, in his bonnet. But in real fact the historian is a product of the hive; he cannot shed, if he would, the coloring matter of his own age, and what the Prime Minister speaks of as individual bias is really the instinct of the herd.

In the attitude of English historians toward the American

Revolution we can find this ebb and flow of opinion. We might wish that Gibbon had lived thirty or a hundred years later, to write the decline and fall of the first British Empire, but actually he did more—he contributed to it; for he sat in the House of Commons and voted, silently but without a pang, for every measure which made that fall final. Let us do him the justice to remember that his views were formed before Lord North put him on the Board of Trade, and though he wrote that North did not deserve "pardon for the past, or confidence for the future," he held tolerably firmly to the view that the cause of government was "in this instance" that of England.

The Rise of Pitt

But in 1784 the younger Pitt came into power—he who had denounced the American war as abominable and murderous—and from that time any "Tory" view of the Revolution would have met with as hopeless a reception in England as in Boston. Here and there an old gentleman lingered on who stood for the King's system, but power had passed to the Reformers and the realists, even among the Tories.

It would be wrong, indeed, to exaggerate the extent to which the English had swallowed their medicine, and thoroughly absorbed the "lesson" of the loss of America; nations cannot, in a day or a generation, unlearn all the maxims which they have always practiced.

Constitutional difficulties were implicit in the very relation of mother country and colony, and must have come to a head if George III had died in the cradle, or if he had lived to be a monument of wisdom. The navigation acts and the system attached to them hung on till the time of Gladstone, and Lord John Russell's irritating mind delighted in making so clear the dilemma of responsible government that he clouded the whole future of another empire.

But the Whigs, Benthamites, and Colonial reformers agreed in condemning George III, and the germ of self-government which Pitt planted in the Canadas grew irresistibly into the tough growth whose existence Elgin had to recognize. It was, besides, out of the question that the dynasty of Victorian historians should concern itself with royal administration.

It was from Lord Macaulay, a great and virile figure, that the Victorian citizen drew his conception of our history, and though he nowhere dealt with the American question directly, his general position sufficiently illustrates the moral he would have drawn. His "History of England" set out to explain the "progress from poverty and barbarism to the highest degrees of opulence and civilization," finding a landmark in "the stand which was made by our forefathers against the House of Stuart." It is a paean of praise "for the authority of law, for the security of property, for the peace of our streets," gratitude for which was due, "under Him who raises and pulls down nations at His pleasure, to the Long Parliament, to the Convention, and to William of Orange."

Version of Washington

The Whig version of English liberties was backed up by a more austere writer in Henry Hallam, whose "Constitutional History," though written in 1827, is still fresh today because it throbs with the cause, "the good old cause," for which Sidney died on the scaffold and for which James Otis and Washington, on this view, also contended.

It was at last applied immediately to America by Macaulay's nephew, Sir George Trevelyan, whose "History of the American Revolution" held the field in England till our own day. Its angle was acute, its moral most dogmatic, its limitations enormous. That severe critic, John Andrew Doyle, described its attitude once for all: "As Malebranche saw all things in God, so Sir George Trevelyan sees the American Revolution in Fox and the Whig party."

Liberalism of the '80s

In the 1880s historical liberalism in England reached, perhaps, its zenith in John Richard Green who, though infinitely more judicial and dispassionate than Macaulay, still imputed to George III on his accession a plan to crush "the republican spirit" of America and to enforce "their dependence upon Britain."

When we reach the age of Seeley, Lecky and Acton we find that the tide of opinion has turned. The change did not consist in any attempt to cover the follies of George III or any other individual; to do the Tory-biased historians justice, they had not —at any time in the century—come to that. Alison's "History of Europe" was a book by which our Tory ancestors swore and even he confessed the "imbecility" of our men on the spot. The highly conservative Stanhope denounced our "measures of aggression."

The highest Tory view of the present day might be found in Sir John Fortescue, and even there we find very solid fact, though taken from only one aspect; George III, he argues, had to deal "not with reasonable men laboring under a legitimate grievance but with revolutionaries, suffering from bad times after a long and exhausting war, and keenly alive to the fact that the removal of the enemy on their borders had rendered them independent of British protection."

No, the real change has been deeper, as any representative passage of the modern school will show. First hear Seeley: "If we imposed taxes upon them, it was to meet the debt which we had incurred in their behalf, and we saw with not unnatural bitterness that we had ourselves enabled our Colonies to do without us, by destroying for their interest the French power in North America." And then the Liberal Lecky: "There were assuredly no other Colonies in the world so favorably situated"—it is a "flagrant misrepresentation to describe the commercial policy of England as exceptionally tyrannical."

Finally I give the high authority of Lord Acton: "There was

no tyranny to be resented. The colonists were in many ways more completely their own masters than Englishmen at home," and "by the rules of right, which had been obeyed till then, England had the better cause." All of which, after all, could be matched from Chief Justice Marshall many years before, who said that "no practical oppression had been experienced" and that Washington's contemporaries had taken arms to resist claims "the presence of which had not been felt."

But once historical studies had come down to earth, they had to go deeper down still, and to strike to the roots of the controversy. They found it, at last, in the old Colonial origins and in the economic and social components of the American people. This meant an effort to comprehend the English administrators, from Clarendon and Locke down to Lord Dartmouth, and the character of Governors like Shirley or Pownall.

The charter liberties of the old Colonies were shown to be real and wide; as Professor Andrewes has said, "British subjects in America had attained, in fact if not in law, an equal political status with British subjects in Great Britain, and their governing bodies had won a position of commanding prominence and authority similar, each in its sphere, to that which the British Parliament had won in the realm." It was found that the commercial code had been constantly amended in favor of America, and had kept for Americans a substantial place in European markets; while the first serious examination of the history of the frontier brought to light British endeavor to protect the Indians.

American Scholars

In all this the lead has been taken by American historians, who first taught Englishmen to understand their own Colonial policy. Lecky and Doyle in England could not alone have restored opinion on this controversy to the proper level; Winsor and Fiske, Channing and Beer, Van Tyne and Andrewes and Morison, these and other American scholars have the chief credit of making this addition to truth, and hence to the world's peace. For an Englishman would have hardly found credit if, for instance, he had written, with Van Tyne, that "the Revolution was on the whole the work of the lower and middle classes," and that in New England "half at least of the wealthy, educated and respected classes" were Loyalists.

It has taken a hundred years for the Anglo-Saxon world to be able to appreciate the conclusion of Professor McIlwain— "The Colonists retained to a marked and unusual degree the traditions of Tudor England. * * * The breach between Colonies and mother country was largely a mutual misunderstanding, based in great part on the fact of this retention of older ideas in the Colonies, after Parliamentary sovereignty had driven them out in the mother country."

The sequence of events is, then, truly described in the words of the Prime Minister, which make our text, but in one respect he understated them; to the best of my belief, no history with "a Tory bias" has been written in England—history worth the name —since the death of Hume.

Suggested Reading

John R. Alden, *A History of the American Revolution,* New York, Alfred A. Knopf, 1969.

Bernard Bailyn, *The Ideological Origins of the American Revolution,* Cambridge, Mass., Harvard University Press, 1967.

Carl Bridenbaugh, *Mitre and Sceptre: Transatlantic Faiths, Ideas, Personalities and Politics, 1689–1775,* New York, Oxford University Press, 1962 (Galaxy paperback).

Elisha P. Douglas, *Rebels and Democrats: The Struggle for Equal Political Rights and Majority Rule During the American Revolution,* Chapel Hill, University of North Carolina Press, 1955 (Quadrangle paperback).

Lawrence H. Gipson, *The Coming of the Revolution, 1763–1775,* New York, Harper, 1954 (Harper Torchbook paperback).

Jack P. Greene, ed., *The Reinterpretation of the American Revolution, 1763–1789,* New York, Harper and Row, 1968.

Merrill Jensen, *The Founding of a Nation: A History of the American Revolution, 1763–1776,* New York, Oxford University Press, 1968.

Lawrence H. Leder, *Liberty and Authority: Early American Political Ideology, 1689–1763,* Chicago, Quadrangle Books, 1968.

Forrest McDonald, *E Pluribus Unum: The Formation of the*

American Republic, 1776–1790, Boston, Houghton Mifflin, 1965 (Pelican paperback).

Charles H. McIlwain, *The American Revolution: A Constitutional Interpretation,* New York, Macmillan, 1923 (Cornell paperback).

Edmund S. Morgan, *The Birth of the Republic, 1763–89,* Chicago, University of Chicago Press, 1956 (Phoenix paperback).

Robert R. Palmer, *The Age of Democratic Revolution,* Princeton, Princeton University Press, 1959.

Eric Robson, *The American Revolution in Its Political and Military Aspects, 1763–1783,* New York, Norton, 1966 (Norton paperback).

R. J. White, *The Age of George III,* New York, Walker, 1968.

Esmond Wright, *Fabric of Freedom, 1763–1800,* New York, Hill and Wang, 1961 (Hill and Wang paperback).

Index

A Note on the Editor

LAWRENCE H. LEDER is the author of *Liberty and Authority: Early American Political Ideology, 1689–1763; The Glorious Revolution in America;* and *Robert Livingston and the Politics of Colonial New York.* He was born in New York City, studied at Long Island University and New York University, and is now Professor of History and chairman of the department at Lehigh University.

New York Times Books
published by Quadrangle Books

American Foreign Policy Since 1945
    edited by Robert A. Divine

American Politics Since 1945
    edited by Richard M. Dalfiume

American Society Since 1945
    edited by William L. O'Neill

Cities in Trouble
    edited by Nathan Glazer

The Meaning of the American Revolution
    edited by Lawrence H. Leder

Modern American Cities
    edited by Ray Ginger

Nazis and Fascists in Europe, 1918-1945
    edited by John Weiss

Available in Paperback and Cloth Editions
Current Catalog On Request